HOW TO TELL

A STORY

and Other Essays

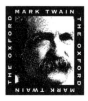

THE OXFORD MARK TWAIN

Shelley Fisher Fishkin, Editor

The Celebrated Jumping Frog of Calaveras County, and Other Sketches
 Introduction: Roy Blount Jr.
 Afterword: Richard Bucci

The Innocents Abroad
 Introduction: Mordecai Richler
 Afterword: David E. E. Sloane

Roughing It
 Introduction: George Plimpton
 Afterword: Henry B. Wonham

The Gilded Age
 Introduction: Ward Just
 Afterword: Gregg Camfield

Sketches, New and Old
 Introduction: Lee Smith
 Afterword: Sherwood Cummings

The Adventures of Tom Sawyer
 Introduction: E. L. Doctorow
 Afterword: Albert E. Stone

A Tramp Abroad
 Introduction: Russell Banks
 Afterword: James S. Leonard

How to
Tell a Story
and Other Essays

Mark Twain

FOREWORD

SHELLEY FISHER FISHKIN

INTRODUCTION

DAVID BRADLEY

AFTERWORD

PASCAL COVICI, JR.

New York   Oxford

OXFORD UNIVERSITY PRESS

1996

OXFORD UNIVERSITY PRESS

Oxford   New York

Athens, Auckland, Bangkok, Bogotá, Bombay

Buenos Aires, Calcutta, Cape Town, Dar es Salaam

Delhi, Florence, Hong Kong, Istanbul, Karachi

Kuala Lumpur, Madras, Madrid, Melbourne

Mexico City, Nairobi, Paris, Singapore

Taipei, Tokyo, Toronto

and associated companies in

Berlin, Ibadan

Copyright © 1996 by

Oxford University Press, Inc.

Introduction © 1996 by David Bradley

Afterword © 1996 by Pascal Covici, Jr.

Text design by Richard Hendel

Composition: David Thorne

Published by

Oxford University Press, Inc.

198 Madison Avenue, New York,

New York 10016

Oxford is a registered trademark of

Oxford University Press

Library of Congress

Cataloging-in-Publication Data

Twain, Mark, 1835–1910.

How to tell a story, and other essays / by Mark

Twain; with an introduction by David Bradley and

an afterword by Pascal Covici, Jr.

p. cm. — (The Oxford Mark Twain)

1. Storytelling. I. Series: Twain, Mark, 1835–1910.

Works. 1996.

PS1322.H6 1996

813'.4—dc20

96-16579

CIP

ISBN 0-19-510149-9 (trade ed.)

ISBN 0-19-511418-3 (lib. ed.)

ISBN 0-19-509088-8 (trade ed. set)

ISBN 0-19-511345-4 (lib. ed. set)

9 8 7 6 5 4 3 2 1

Printed in the United States of America

on acid-free paper

FRONTISPIECE

Samuel L. Clemens is seen here in a photograph
taken by Alfred Ellis in London in 1897, the year he
published *How to Tell a Story and Other Essays*.
(The Mark Twain House, Hartford, Connecticut)

CONTENTS

EDITOR'S NOTE

The Oxford Mark Twain consists of twenty-nine volumes of facsimiles of the first American editions of Mark Twain's works, with an editor's foreword, new introductions, afterwords, notes on the texts, and essays on the illustrations in volumes with artwork. The facsimiles have been reproduced from the originals unaltered, except that blank pages in the front and back of the books have been omitted, and any seriously damaged or missing pages have been replaced by pages from other first editions (as indicated in the notes on the texts).

In the foreword, introduction, afterword, and essays on the illustrations, the titles of Mark Twain's works have been capitalized according to modern conventions, as have the names of characters (except where otherwise indicated). In the case of discrepancies between the title of a short story, essay, or sketch as it appears in the original table of contents and as it appears on its own title page, the title page has been followed. The parenthetical numbers in the introduction, afterwords, and illustration essays are page references to the facsimiles.

FOREWORD

Shelley Fisher Fishkin

Samuel Clemens entered the world and left it with Halley's Comet, little dreaming that generations hence Halley's Comet would be less famous than Mark Twain. He has been called the American Cervantes, our Homer, our Tolstoy, our Shakespeare, our Rabelais. Ernest Hemingway maintained that "all modern American literature comes from one book by Mark Twain called *Huckleberry Finn*." President Franklin Delano Roosevelt got the phrase "New Deal" from *A Connecticut Yankee in King Arthur's Court*. *The Gilded Age* gave an entire era its name. "The future historian of America," wrote George Bernard Shaw to Samuel Clemens, "will find your works as indispensable to him as a French historian finds the political tracts of Voltaire."[1]

There is a Mark Twain Bank in St. Louis, a Mark Twain Diner in Jackson Heights, New York, a Mark Twain Smoke Shop in Lakeland, Florida. There are Mark Twain Elementary Schools in Albuquerque, Dayton, Seattle, and Sioux Falls. Mark Twain's image peers at us from advertisements for Bass Ale (his drink of choice was Scotch), for a gas company in Tennessee, a hotel in the nation's capital, a cemetery in California.

Ubiquitous though his name and image may be, Mark Twain is in no danger of becoming a petrified icon. On the contrary: Mark Twain lives. *Huckleberry Finn* is "the most taught novel, most taught long work, and most taught piece of American literature" in American schools from junior high to the graduate level.[2] Hundreds of Twain impersonators appear in theaters, trade shows, and shopping centers in every region of the country.[3] Scholars publish hundreds of articles as well as books about Twain every year, and he is the subject of daily exchanges on the Internet. A journalist somewhere in the world finds a reason to quote Twain just about every day. Television series such as *Bonanza*, *Star Trek: The Next Generation*, and *Cheers* broadcast episodes that feature Mark Twain as a character. Hollywood screenwriters regularly produce movies inspired by his works, and writers of mysteries and science fiction continue to weave him into their plots.[4]

A century after the American Revolution sent shock waves throughout Europe, it took Mark Twain to explain to Europeans and to his countrymen alike what that revolution had wrought. He probed the significance of this new land and its new citizens, and identified what it was in the Old World that America abolished and rejected. The founding fathers had thought through the political dimensions of making a new society; Mark Twain took on the challenge of interpreting the social and cultural life of the United States for those outside its borders as well as for those who were living the changes he discerned.

Americans may have constructed a new society in the eighteenth century, but they articulated what they had done in voices that were largely inter-changeable with those of Englishmen until well into the nineteenth century. Mark Twain became the voice of the new land, the leading translator of what and who the "American" was — and, to a large extent, is. Frances Trollope's *Domestic Manners of the Americans*, a best-seller in England, Hector St. John de Crèvecoeur's *Letters from an American Farmer*, and Tocqueville's *Democracy in America* all tried to explain America to Europeans. But Twain did more than that: he allowed European readers to *experience* this strange "new world." And he gave his countrymen the tools to do two things they had not quite had the confidence to do before. He helped them stand before the cultural icons of the Old World unembarrassed, unashamed of America's lack of palaces and shrines, proud of its brash practicality and bold inventiveness, unafraid to reject European models of "civilization" as tainted or corrupt. And he also helped them recognize their own insularity, boorishness, arrogance, or ignorance, and laugh at it — the first step toward transcending it and becoming more "civilized," in the best European sense of the word.

Twain often strikes us as more a creature of our time than of his. He appreciated the importance and the complexity of mass tourism and public relations, fields that would come into their own in the twentieth century but were only fledgling enterprises in the nineteenth. He explored the liberating potential of humor and the dynamics of friendship, parenting, and marriage. He narrowed the gap between "popular" and "high" culture, and he meditated on the enigmas of personal and national identity. Indeed, it would be difficult to find an issue on the horizon today that Twain did not touch on somewhere in his work. Heredity versus environment? Animal rights? The boundaries of gender? The place of black voices in the cultural heritage of the United States? Twain was there.

With startling prescience and characteristic grace and wit, he zeroed in on many of the key challenges — political, social, and technological — that would face his country and the world for the next hundred years: the challenge of race relations in a society founded on both chattel slavery and ideals of equality, and the intractable problem of racism in American life; the potential of new technologies to transform our lives in ways that can be both exhilarating and terrifying — as well as unpredictable; the problem of imperialism and the difficulties entailed in getting rid of it. But he never lost sight of the most basic challenge of all: each man or woman's struggle for integrity in the face of the seductions of power, status, and material things.

Mark Twain's unerring sense of the right word and not its second cousin taught people to pay attention when he spoke, in person or in print. He said things that were smart and things that were wise, and he said them incomparably well. He defined the rhythms of our prose and the contours of our moral map. He saw our best and our worst, our extravagant promise and our stunning failures, our comic foibles and our tragic flaws. Throughout the world he is viewed as the most distinctively American of American authors — and as one of the most universal. He is assigned in classrooms in Naples, Riyadh, Belfast, and Beijing, and has been a major influence on twentieth-century writers from Argentina to Nigeria to Japan. The Oxford Mark Twain celebrates the versatility and vitality of this remarkable writer.

The Oxford Mark Twain reproduces the first American editions of Mark Twain's books published during his lifetime.[5] By encountering Twain's works in their original format — typography, layout, order of contents, and illustrations — readers today can come a few steps closer to the literary artifacts that entranced and excited readers when the books first appeared. Twain approved of and to a greater or lesser degree supervised the publication of all of this material.[6] The Mark Twain House in Hartford, Connecticut, generously loaned us its originals.[7] When more than one copy of a first American edition was available, Robert H. Hirst, general editor of the Mark Twain Project, in cooperation with Marianne Curling, curator of the Mark Twain House (and Jeffrey Kaimowitz, head of Rare Books for the Watkinson Library of Trinity College, Hartford, where the Mark Twain House collection is kept), guided our decision about which one to use.[8] As a set, the volumes also contain more than eighty essays commissioned especially for The Oxford Mark Twain, in which distinguished contributors reassess Twain's achievement as a writer and his place in the cultural conversation that he did so much to shape.

Each volume of The Oxford Mark Twain is introduced by a leading American, Canadian, or British writer who responds to Twain — often in a very personal way — as a fellow writer. Novelists, journalists, humorists, columnists, fabulists, poets, playwrights — these writers tell us what Twain taught them and what in his work continues to speak to them. Reading Twain's books, both famous and obscure, they reflect on the genesis of his art and the characteristics of his style, the themes he illuminated, and the aesthetic strategies he pioneered. Individually and collectively their contributions testify to the place Mark Twain holds in the hearts of readers of all kinds and temperaments.

Scholars whose work has shaped our view of Twain in the academy today have written afterwords to each volume, with suggestions for further reading. Their essays give us a sense of what was going on in Twain's life when he wrote the book at hand, and of how that book fits into his career. They explore how each book reflects and refracts contemporary events, and they show Twain responding to literary and social currents of the day, variously accepting, amplifying, modifying, and challenging prevailing paradigms. Sometimes they argue that works previously dismissed as quirky or eccentric departures actually address themes at the heart of Twain's work from the start. And as they bring new perspectives to Twain's composition strategies in familiar texts, several scholars see experiments in form where others saw only form-lessness, method where prior critics saw only madness. In addition to eluci-dating the work's historical and cultural context, the afterwords provide an overview of responses to each book from its first appearance to the present.

Most of Mark Twain's books involved more than Mark Twain's words: unique illustrations. The parodic visual send-ups of "high culture" that Twain himself drew for *A Tramp Abroad*, the sketch of financial manipulator Jay Gould as a greedy and sadistic "Slave Driver" in *A Connecticut Yankee in King Arthur's Court*, and the memorable drawings of Eve in *Eve's Diary* all helped Twain's books to be sold, read, discussed, and preserved. In their es-says for each volume that contains artwork, Beverly R. David and Ray Sapirstein highlight the significance of the sketches, engravings, and pho-tographs in the first American editions of Mark Twain's works, and tell us what is known about the public response to them.

The Oxford Mark Twain invites us to read some relatively neglected works by Twain in the company of some of the most engaging literary figures of our time. Roy Blount Jr., for example, riffs in a deliciously Twain-like manner on "An Item Which the Editor Himself Could Not Understand," which may well rank as one of the least-known pieces Twain ever published. Bobbie Ann Mason celebrates the "mad energy" of Twain's most obscure comic novel, *The American Claimant*, in which the humor "hurtles beyond tall tale into simon-pure absurdity."[9] Garry Wills finds that *Christian Science* "gets us very close to the heart of American culture." Lee Smith reads "Political Economy" as a sharp and funny essay on language. Walter Mosley sees "The Stolen White Elephant," a story "reduced to a series of ridiculous telegrams related by an untrustworthy narrator caught up in an adventure that is as impossible as it is ludicrous," as a stunningly compact and economical satire of a world we still recognize as our own. Anne Bernays returns to "The Private History of a Campaign That Failed" and finds "an antiwar manifesto that is also confession, dramatic monologue, a plea for understanding and absolution, and a romp that gradually turns into atrocity even as we watch." After revisiting Captain Stormfield's heaven, Frederik Pohl finds that there "is no imaginable place more pleasant to spend eternity." Indeed, Pohl writes, "one would almost be willing to die to enter it."

While less familiar works receive fresh attention in The Oxford Mark Twain, new light is cast on the best-known works as well. Judith Martin ("Miss Manners") points out that it is by reading a court etiquette book that Twain's pauper learns how to behave as a proper prince. As important as etiquette may be in the palace, Martin notes, it is even more important in the slums.

> That etiquette is a sorer point with the ruffians in the street than with the proud dignitaries of the prince's court may surprise some readers. As in our own streets, etiquette is always a more volatile subject among those who cannot count on being treated with respect than among those who have the power to command deference.

And taking a fresh look at *Adventures of Huckleberry Finn,* Toni Morrison writes,

> much of the novel's genius lies in its quiescence, the silences that pervade it and give it a porous quality that is by turns brooding and soothing. It lies in ... the subdued images in which the repetition of a simple word, such as "lonesome," tolls like an evening bell; the moments when nothing is said, when scenes and incidents swell the heart unbearably precisely because unarticulated, and force an act of imagination almost against the will.

Engaging Mark Twain as one writer to another, several contributors to The Oxford Mark Twain offer new insights into the processes by which his books came to be. Russell Banks, for example, reads *A Tramp Abroad* as "an important revision of Twain's incomplete first draft of *Huckleberry Finn*, a second draft, if you will, which in turn made possible the third and final draft." Erica Jong suggests that *1601*, a freewheeling parody of Elizabethan manners and mores, written during the same summer Twain began *Huckleberry Finn*, served as "a warm-up for his creative process" and "primed the pump for other sorts of freedom of expression." And Justin Kaplan suggests that "one of the transcendent figures standing behind and shaping" *Joan of Arc* was Ulysses S. Grant, whose memoirs Twain had recently published, and who, like Joan, had risen unpredictably "from humble and obscure origins" to become a "military genius" endowed with "the gift of command, a natural eloquence, and an equally natural reserve."

As a number of contributors note, Twain was a man ahead of his times. *The Gilded Age* was the first "Washington novel," Ward Just tells us, because "Twain was the first to see the possibilities that had eluded so many others." Commenting on *The Tragedy of Pudd'nhead Wilson*, Sherley Anne Williams observes that "Twain's argument about the power of environment in shaping character runs directly counter to prevailing sentiment where the negro was concerned." Twain's fictional technology, wildly fanciful by the standards of his day, predicts developments we take for granted in ours. DNA cloning, fax machines, and photocopiers are all prefigured, Bobbie Ann Mason tells us, in *The American Claimant*. Cynthia Ozick points out that the "telelectrophonoscope" we meet in "From the 'London Times' of 1904" is suspiciously like what we know as "television." And Malcolm Bradbury suggests that in the "phrenophones" of "Mental Telegraphy" "the Internet was born."

Twain turns out to have been remarkably prescient about political affairs as well. Kurt Vonnegut sees in *A Connecticut Yankee* a chilling foreshadowing (or perhaps a projection from the Civil War) of "all the high-tech atrocities which followed, and which follow still." Cynthia Ozick suggests that "The Man That Corrupted Hadleyburg," along with some of the other pieces collected under that title — many of them written when Twain lived in a Vienna ruled by Karl Lueger, a demagogue Adolf Hitler would later idolize — shoot up moral flares that shed an eerie light on the insidious corruption, prejudice, and hatred that reached bitter fruition under the Third Reich. And Twain's portrait in this book of "the dissolving Austria-Hungary of the 1890s," in Ozick's view, presages not only the Sarajevo that would erupt in 1914 but also "the disintegrated components of the former Yugoslavia" and "the *fin-de-siècle* Sarajevo of our own moment."

Despite their admiration for Twain's ambitious reach and scope, contributors to The Oxford Mark Twain also recognize his limitations. Mordecai Richler, for example, thinks that "the early pages of *Innocents Abroad* suffer from being a tad broad, proffering more burlesque than inspired satire," perhaps because Twain was "trying too hard for knee-slappers." Charles Johnson notes that the Young Man in Twain's philosophical dialogue about free will and determinism (*What Is Man?*) "caves in far too soon," failing to challenge what through late-twentieth-century eyes looks like "pseudoscience" and suspect essentialism in the Old Man's arguments.

Some contributors revisit their first encounters with Twain's works, recalling what surprised or intrigued them. When David Bradley came across "Fenimore Cooper's Literary Offences" in his college library, he "did not at first realize that Twain was being his usual ironic self with all this business about the 'nineteen rules governing literary art in the domain of romantic fiction,' but by the time I figured out there was no such list outside Twain's own head, I had decided that the rules made *sense.* . . . It seemed to me they were a pretty good blueprint for writing — Negro writing included." Sherley Anne Williams remembers that part of what attracted her to *Pudd'nhead Wilson* when she first read it thirty years ago was "that Twain, writing at the end of the nineteenth century, could imagine negroes as characters, albeit white ones, who actually thought for and of themselves, whose actions were the product of their thinking rather than the spontaneous ephemera of physical instincts that stereotype assigned to blacks." Frederik Pohl recalls his first reading of *Huckleberry Finn* as "a watershed event" in his life, the first book he read as a child in which "bad people" ceased to exercise a monopoly on doing "bad things." In *Huckleberry Finn* "some seriously bad things — things like the possession and mistreatment of black slaves, like stealing and lying, even like killing other people in duels — were quite often done by people who not only thought of themselves as exemplarily moral but, by any other standards I knew how to apply, actually *were* admirable citizens." The world that

Tom and Huck lived in, Pohl writes, "was filled with complexities and con-tradictions," and resembled "the world I appeared to be living in myself."

Other contributors explore their more recent encounters with Twain, ex-plaining why they have revised their initial responses to his work. For Toni Morrison, parts of *Huckleberry Finn* that she "once took to be deliberate eva-sions, stumbles even, or a writer's impatience with his or her material," now strike her "as otherwise: as entrances, crevices, gaps, seductive invitations flashing the possibility of meaning. Unarticulated eddies that encourage div-ing into the novel's undertow — the real place where writer captures reader." One such "eddy" is the imprisonment of Jim on the Phelps farm. Instead of dismissing this portion of the book as authorial bungling, as she once did, Morrison now reads it as Twain's commentary on the 1880s, a period that "saw the collapse of civil rights for blacks," a time when "the nation, as well as Tom Sawyer, was deferring Jim's freedom in agonizing play." Morrison be-lieves that Americans in the 1880s were attempting "to bury the combustible issues Twain raised in his novel," and that those who try to kick Huck Finn out of school in the 1990s are doing the same: "The cyclical attempts to re-move the novel from classrooms extend Jim's captivity on into each genera-tion of readers."

Although imitation-Hemingway and imitation-Faulkner writing contests draw hundreds of entries annually, no one has ever tried to mount a faux-Twain competition. Why? Perhaps because Mark Twain's voice is too much a part of who we are and how we speak even today. Roy Blount Jr. suggests that it is impossible, "at least for an American writer, to parody Mark Twain. It would be like doing an impression of your father or mother: he or she is al-ready there in your voice."

Twain's style is examined and celebrated in The Oxford Mark Twain by fellow writers who themselves have struggled with the nuances of words, the structure of sentences, the subtleties of point of view, and the trickiness of opening lines. Bobbie Ann Mason observes, for example, that "Twain loved the sound of words and he knew how to string them by sound, like different shades of one color: 'The earl's barbaric eye,' 'the Usurping Earl,' 'a double-dyed humbug.'" Twain "relied on the punch of plain words" to show writers how to move beyond the "wordy romantic rubbish" so prevalent in nineteenth-century fiction, Mason says; he "was one of the first writers in America to deflower literary language." Lee Smith believes that "American writers have benefited as much from the way Mark Twain opened up the possibilities of first-person narration as we have from his use of vernacular language." (She feels that "the ghost of Mark Twain was hovering someplace in the background" when she decided to write her novel *Oral History* from the standpoint of multiple first-person narrators.) Frederick Busch maintains that "A Dog's Tale" "boasts one of the great opening sentences" of all time: "My father was a St. Bernard, my mother was a collie, but I am a Presbyterian." And Ursula Le Guin marvels at the ingenuity of the following sentence that she encounters in *Extracts from Adam's Diary*.

. . . This made her sorry for the creatures which live in there, which she calls fish, for she continues to fasten names on to things that don't need them and don't come when they are called by them, which is a matter of no consequence to her, as she is such a numskull anyway; so she got a lot of them out and brought them in last night and put them in my bed to keep warm, but I have noticed them now and then all day, and I don't see that they are any happier there than they were before, only quieter.[10]

Le Guin responds,

Now, that is a pure Mark-Twain-tour-de-force sentence, covering an immense amount of territory in an effortless, aimless ramble that seems to be heading nowhere in particular and ends up with breathtaking accuracy at the gold mine. Any sensible child would find that funny, perhaps not following all its divagations but delighted by the swing of it, by the word "numskull," by the idea of putting fish in the bed; and as that child grew older and reread it, its reward would only grow; and if that grown-up child had to write an essay on the piece and therefore earnestly studied and pored over this sentence, she would end up in unmitigated admiration of its vocabulary, syntax, pacing, sense, and rhythm, above all the beautiful timing of the last two words; and she would, and she does, still find it funny.

The fish surface again in a passage that Gore Vidal calls to our attention, from *Following the Equator*: "'The Whites always mean well when they take human fish out of the ocean and try to make them dry and warm and happy and comfortable in a chicken coop,' which is how, through civilization, they did away with many of the original inhabitants. Lack of empathy is a principal theme in Twain's meditations on race and empire."

Indeed, empathy — and its lack — is a principal theme in virtually all of Twain's work, as contributors frequently note. Nat Hentoff quotes the following thoughts from Huck in *Tom Sawyer Abroad*:

> I see a bird setting on a dead limb of a high tree, singing with its head tilted back and its mouth open, and before I thought I fired, and his song stopped and he fell straight down from the limb, all limp like a rag, and I run and picked him up and he was dead, and his body was warm in my hand, and his head rolled about this way and that, like his neck was broke, and there was a little white skin over his eyes, and one little drop of blood on the side of his head; and laws! I could n't see nothing more for the tears; and I hain't never murdered no creature since that war n't doing me no harm, and I ain't going to.[11]

"The Humane Society," Hentoff writes, "has yet to say anything as powerful — and lasting."

Readers of The Oxford Mark Twain will have the pleasure of revisiting Twain's Mississippi landmarks alongside Willie Morris, whose own lower Mississippi Valley boyhood gives him a special sense of connection to Twain. Morris knows firsthand the mosquitoes described in *Life on the Mississippi* — so colossal that "two of them could whip a dog" and "four of them could hold a man down"; in Morris's own hometown they were so large during the flood season that "local wags said they wore wristwatches." Morris's Yazoo City and Twain's Hannibal shared a "rough-hewn democracy . . . complicated by all the visible textures of caste and class, . . . harmless boyhood fun and mischief right along with . . . rank hypocrisies, churchgoing sanctimonies, racial hatred, entrenched and unrepentant greed."

For the West of Mark Twain's *Roughing It*, readers will have George Plimpton as their guide. "What a group these newspapermen were!" Plimpton writes about Twain and his friends Dan De Quille and Joe Goodman in Virginia City, Nevada. "Their roisterous carryings-on bring to mind the kind of frat-house enthusiasm one associates with college humor magazines like the *Harvard Lampoon*." Malcolm Bradbury examines Twain as "a living example of what made the American so different from the European." And Hal Holbrook, who has interpreted Mark Twain on stage for some forty years, describes how Twain "played" during the civil rights movement, during the Vietnam War, during the Gulf War, and in Prague on the eve of the demise of Communism.

Why do we continue to read Mark Twain? What draws us to him? His wit? His compassion? His humor? His bravura? His humility? His understanding of who and what we are in those parts of our being that we rarely open to view? Our sense that he knows we can do better than we do? Our sense that he knows we can't? E. L. Doctorow tells us that children are attracted to *Tom Sawyer* because in this book "the young reader confirms his own hope that no matter how troubled his relations with his elders may be, beneath all their disapproval is their underlying love for him, constant and steadfast." Readers in general, Arthur Miller writes, value Twain's "insights into America's always uncertain moral life and its shifting but everlasting hypocrisies"; we appreciate the fact that he "is not using his alienation from the public illusions of his hour in order to reject the country implicitly as though he could live without it, but manifestly in order to correct it." Perhaps we keep reading Mark Twain because, in Miller's words, he "wrote much more like a father than a son. He doesn't seem to be sitting in class taunting the teacher but standing at the head of it challenging his students to acknowledge their own humanity, that is, their immemorial attraction to the untrue."

Mark Twain entered the public eye at a time when many of his countrymen considered "American culture" an oxymoron; he died four years before a world conflagration that would lead many to question whether the contradiction in terms was not "European civilization" instead. In between he worked in journalism, printing, steamboating, mining, lecturing, publishing, and editing, in virtually every region of the country. He tried his hand at humorous sketches, social satire, historical novels, children's books, poetry, drama, science fiction, mysteries, romance, philosophy, travelogue, memoir, polemic, and several genres no one had ever seen before or has ever seen since. He invented a self-pasting scrapbook, a history game, a vest strap, and a gizmo for keeping bed sheets tucked in; he invested in machines and processes designed to revolutionize typesetting and engraving, and in a food supplement called "Plasmon." Along the way he cheerfully impersonated himself and prior versions of himself for doting publics on five continents while playing out a charming rags-to-riches story followed by a devastating riches-to-rags story followed by yet another great American comeback. He had a long-running real-life engagement in a sumptuous comedy of manners, and then in a real-life tragedy not of his own design: during the last fourteen years of his life almost everyone he ever loved was taken from him by disease and death.

Mark Twain has indelibly shaped our views of who and what the United States is as a nation and of who and what we might become. He understood the nostalgia for a "simpler" past that increased as that past receded — and he saw through the nostalgia to a past that was just as complex as the present. He recognized better than we did ourselves our potential for greatness and our potential for disaster. His fictions brilliantly illuminated the world in which he lived, changing it — and us — in the process. He knew that our feet often danced to tunes that had somehow remained beyond our hearing; with perfect pitch he played them back to us.

My mother read *Tom Sawyer* to me as a bedtime story when I was eleven. I thought Huck and Tom could be a lot of fun, but I dismissed Becky Thatcher as a bore. When I was twelve I invested a nickel at a local garage sale in a book that contained short pieces by Mark Twain. That was where I met Twain's Eve. Now, *that's* more like it, I decided, pleased to meet a female character I could identify *with* instead of against. Eve had spunk. Even if she got a lot wrong, you had to give her credit for trying. "The Man That Corrupted

Hadleyburg" left me giddy with satisfaction: none of my adolescent reveries of getting even with my enemies were half as neat as the plot of the man who got back at that town. "How I Edited an Agricultural Paper" set me off in uncontrollable giggles.

People sometimes told me that I looked like Huck Finn. "It's the freckles," they'd explain — not explaining anything at all. I didn't read *Huckleberry Finn* until junior year in high school in my English class. It was the fall of 1965. I was living in a small town in Connecticut. I expected a sequel to *Tom Sawyer*. So when the teacher handed out the books and announced our assignment, my jaw dropped: "Write a paper on how Mark Twain used irony to attack racism in *Huckleberry Finn*."

The year before, the bodies of three young men who had gone to Mississippi to help blacks register to vote — James Chaney, Andrew Goodman, and Michael Schwerner — had been found in a shallow grave; a group of white segregationists (the county sheriff among them) had been arrested in connection with the murders. America's inner cities were simmering with pent-up rage that began to explode in the summer of 1965, when riots in Watts left thirty-four people dead. None of this made any sense to me. I was confused, angry, certain that there was something missing from the news stories I read each day: the why. Then I met Pap Finn. And the Phelpses.

Pap Finn, Huck tells us, "had been drunk over in town" and "was just all mud." He erupts into a drunken tirade about "a free nigger . . . from Ohio — a mulatter, most as white as a white man," with "the whitest shirt on you ever see, too, and the shiniest hat; and there ain't a man in town that's got as fine clothes as what he had."

> . . . they said he was a p'fessor in a college, and could talk all kinds of languages, and knowed everything. And that ain't the wust. They said he could *vote*, when he was at home. Well, that let me out. Thinks I, what is the country a-coming to? It was 'lection day, and I was just about to go and vote, myself, if I warn't too drunk to get there; but when they told me there was a State in this country where they'd let that nigger vote, I drawed out. I says I'll never vote agin. Them's the very words I said. . . . And to see the

cool way of that nigger — why, he wouldn't a give me the road if I hadn't shoved him out o' the way.[12]

Later on in the novel, when the runaway slave Jim gives up his freedom to nurse a wounded Tom Sawyer, a white doctor testifies to the stunning altruism of his actions. The Phelpses and their neighbors, all fine, upstanding, well-meaning, churchgoing folk,

> agreed that Jim had acted very well, and was deserving to have some notice took of it, and reward. So every one of them promised, right out and hearty, that they wouldn't curse him no more.
>
> Then they come out and locked him up. I hoped they was going to say he could have one or two of the chains took off, because they was rotten heavy, or could have meat and greens with his bread and water, but they didn't think of it.[13]

Why did the behavior of these people tell me more about why Watts burned than anything I had read in the daily paper? And why did a drunk Pap Finn railing against a black college professor from Ohio whose vote was as good as his own tell me more about white anxiety over black political power than anything I had seen on the evening news?

Mark Twain knew that there was nothing, absolutely *nothing*, a black man could do — including selflessly sacrificing his freedom, the only thing of value he had — that would make white society see beyond the color of his skin. And Mark Twain knew that depicting racists with chilling accuracy would expose the viciousness of their world view like nothing else could. It was an insight echoed some eighty years after Mark Twain penned Pap Finn's rantings about the black professor, when Malcolm X famously asked, "Do you know what white racists call black Ph.D.'s?" and answered, "'*Nigger!*'"[14]

Mark Twain taught me things I needed to know. He taught me to understand the raw racism that lay behind what I saw on the evening news. He taught me that the most well-meaning people can be hurtful and myopic. He taught me to recognize the supreme irony of a country founded in freedom that continued to deny freedom to so many of its citizens. Every time I hear of another effort to kick Huck Finn out of school somewhere, I recall everything that Mark Twain taught *this* high school junior, and I find myself jumping into the fray.[15] I remember the black high school student who called CNN during the phone-in portion of a 1985 debate between Dr. John Wallace, a black educator spearheading efforts to ban the book, and myself. She accused Dr. Wallace of insulting her and all black high school students by suggesting they weren't smart enough to understand Mark Twain's irony. And I recall the black cameraman on the *CBS Morning News* who came up to me after he finished shooting another debate between Dr. Wallace and myself. He said he had never read the book by Mark Twain that we had been arguing about — but now he really wanted to. One thing that puzzled him, though, was why a white woman was defending it and a black man was attacking it, because as far as he could see from what we'd been saying, the book made whites look pretty bad.

As I came to understand *Huckleberry Finn* and *Pudd'nhead Wilson* as commentaries on the era now known as the nadir of American race relations, those books pointed me toward the world recorded in nineteenth-century black newspapers and periodicals and in fiction by Mark Twain's black contemporaries. My investigation of the role black voices and traditions played in shaping Mark Twain's art helped make me aware of their role in shaping all of American culture.[16] My research underlined for me the importance of changing the stories we tell about who we are to reflect the realities of what we've been.[17]

Ever since our encounter in high school English, Mark Twain has shown me the potential of American literature and American history to illuminate each other. Rarely have I found a contradiction or complexity we grapple with as a nation that Mark Twain had not puzzled over as well. He insisted on taking America seriously. And he insisted on *not* taking America seriously: "I think that there is but a single specialty with us, only one thing that can be called by the wide name 'American,'" he once wrote. "That is the national devotion to ice-water."[18]

Mark Twain threw back at us our dreams and our denial of those dreams, our greed, our goodness, our ambition, and our laziness, all rattling around together in that vast echo chamber of our talk — that sharp, spunky American talk that Mark Twain figured out how to write down without robbing it of its energy and immediacy. Talk shaped by voices that the official arbiters of "culture" deemed of no importance — voices of children, voices of slaves, voices of servants, voices of ordinary people. Mark Twain listened. And he made us listen. To the stories he told us, and to the truths they conveyed. He still has a lot to say that we need to hear.

Mark Twain lives — in our libraries, classrooms, homes, theaters, movie houses, streets, and most of all in our speech. His optimism energizes us, his despair sobers us, and his willingness to keep wrestling with the hilarious and horrendous complexities of it all keeps us coming back for more. As the twenty-first century approaches, may he continue to goad us, chasten us, delight us, berate us, and cause us to erupt in unrestrained laughter in unexpected places.

NOTES

1. Ernest Hemingway, *Green Hills of Africa* (New York: Charles Scribner's Sons, 1935), 22. George Bernard Shaw to Samuel L. Clemens, July 3, 1907, quoted in Albert Bigelow Paine, *Mark Twain: A Biography* (New York: Harper and Brothers, 1912), 3:1398.

2. Allen Carey-Webb, "Racism and *Huckleberry Finn*: Censorship, Dialogue and Change," *English Journal* 82, no. 7 (November 1993):22.

3. See Louis J. Budd, "Impersonators," in J. R. LeMaster and James D. Wilson, eds., *The Mark Twain Encyclopedia* (New York: Garland Publishing Company, 1993), 389-91.

4. See Shelley Fisher Fishkin, "Ripples and Reverberations," part 3 of *Lighting Out for the Territory: Reflections on Mark Twain and American Culture* (New York: Oxford University Press, 1996).

5. There are two exceptions. Twain published chapters from his autobiography in the *North American Review* in 1906 and 1907, but this material was not published in book form in Twain's lifetime; our volume reproduces the material as it appeared in the *North American Review*. The other exception is our final volume, *Mark Twain's Speeches*, which appeared two months after Twain's death in 1910.

An unauthorized handful of copies of *1601* was privately printed by an Alexander Gunn of Cleveland at the instigation of Twain's friend John Hay in 1880. The first American edition authorized by Mark Twain, however, was printed at the United States Military Academy at West Point in 1882; that is the edition reproduced here.

XXVIII : SHELLEY FISHER FISHKIN

It should further be noted that four volumes — *The Stolen White Elephant and Other Detective Stories, Following the Equator and Anti-imperialist Essays, The Diaries of Adam and Eve*, and *1601, and Is Shakespeare Dead?* — bind together material originally published separately. In each case the first American edition of the material is the version that has been reproduced, always in its entirety. Because Twain constantly recycled and repackaged previously published works in his collections of short pieces, a certain amount of duplication is unavoidable. We have selected volumes with an eye toward keeping this duplication to a minimum.

Even the twenty-nine-volume Oxford Mark Twain has had to leave much out. No edition of Twain can ever claim to be "complete," for the man was too prolix, and the file drawers of both ephemera and as yet unpublished texts are deep.

6. With the possible exception of *Mark Twain's Speeches*. Some scholars suspect Twain knew about this book and may have helped shape it, although no hard evidence to that effect has yet surfaced. Twain's involvement in the production process varied greatly from book to book. For a fuller sense of authorial intention, scholars will continue to rely on the superb definitive editions of Twain's works produced by the Mark Twain Project at the University of California at Berkeley as they become available. Dense with annotation documenting textual emendation and related issues, these editions add immeasurably to our understanding of Mark Twain and the genesis of his works.

7. Except for a few titles that were not in its collection. The American Antiquarian Society in Worcester, Massachusetts, provided the first edition of *King Leopold's Soliloquy*; the Elmer Holmes Bobst Library of New York University furnished the 1906–7 volumes of the *North American Review* in which *Chapters from My Autobiography* first appeared; the Harry Ransom Humanities Research Center at the University of Texas at Austin made their copy of the West Point edition of *1601* available; and the Mark Twain Project provided the first edition of *Extract from Captain Stormfield's Visit to Heaven*.

8. The specific copy photographed for Oxford's facsimile edition is indicated in a note on the text at the end of each volume.

9. All quotations from contemporary writers in this essay are taken from their introductions to the volumes of The Oxford Mark Twain, and the quotations from Mark Twain's works are taken from the texts reproduced in The Oxford Mark Twain.

10. *The Diaries of Adam and Eve*, The Oxford Mark Twain [hereafter OMT] (New York: Oxford University Press, 1996), p. 33.

11. *Tom Sawyer Abroad*, OMT, p. 74.

12. *Adventures of Huckleberry Finn*, OMT, p. 49–50.

13. Ibid., p. 358.

14. Malcolm X, *The Autobiography of Malcolm X*, with the assistance of Alex Haley (New York: Grove Press, 1965), p. 284.

15. I do not mean to minimize the challenge of teaching this difficult novel, a challenge for which all teachers may not feel themselves prepared. Elsewhere I have developed some concrete strategies for approaching the book in the classroom, including teaching it in the context of the history of American race relations and alongside books by black writers. See Shelley Fisher Fishkin, "Teaching *Huckleberry Finn*," in James S. Leonard, ed., *Making Mark Twain Work in the Classroom* (Durham: Duke University Press, forthcoming). See also Shelley Fisher Fishkin, *Was Huck Black? Mark Twain and African-American Voices* (New York: Oxford University Press, 1993), pp. 106–8, and a curriculum kit in preparation at the Mark Twain House in Hartford, containing teaching suggestions from myself, David Bradley, Jocelyn Chadwick-Joshua, James Miller, and David E. E. Sloane.

16. See Fishkin, *Was Huck Black?* See also Fishkin, "Interrogating 'Whiteness,' Complicating 'Blackness': Remapping American Culture," in Henry Wonham, ed., *Criticism and the Color Line: Desegregating American Literary Studies* (New Brunswick: Rutgers UP, 1996), pp. 251–90 and in shortened form in *American Quarterly* 47, no. 3 (September 1995):428–66.

17. I explore the roots of my interest in Mark Twain and race at greater length in an essay entitled "Changing the Story," in Jeffrey Rubin-Dorsky and Shelley Fisher Fishkin, eds., *People of the Book: Thirty Scholars Reflect on Their Jewish Identity* (Madison: U of Wisconsin Press, 1996), pp. 47–63.

18. "What Paul Bourget Thinks of Us," *How to Tell a Story and Other Essays*, OMT, p. 197.

INTRODUCTION

David Bradley

I was one month shy of ten years old when I first saw Mark Twain. He was a spade.

It was early August of 1960, a hot, humid, dusty Sunday afternoon. I was sitting on the screened-in side porch, reading the Old Testament, when my mother came out and suggested that she and I play a game.

This may seem quite ordinary, but it shocked me right down to the soles of my Red Ball Jets, for mine was a religious family, by both faith and profession. My father was a minister of the African Methodist Episcopal Zion Church, as was his father, and his father before him. That first father had been a slave, and one of my more eccentric cousins claimed that before him had come several plantation jacklegs and before them a long line of West African conjurers. Though my clan's Elders — Grandmother, Eldest Uncle, Father — doubted the shamanic speculation (in their opinion 'twas mercy brought us from our pagan land and taught our souls to understand salvation), they didn't mind the idea that we had preached the Word even when we were in chains, for they took great pride in saying that at least one male in each of our generations had been Called by Jehovah. And as I was the only male in my generation, and more, a son born to my father's second wife after much prayer and many years of barrenness, they made sure I ciphered the syllogism, saw my destiny as manifest, and worked to keep my heart open to and my soul worthy of the Call.

My grandmother was principal in this instruction. She believed a Call could only come from God, and so never expressed an expectation, but when I was very young she would put aside her knitting, take me onto her ancient lap — she was in her eighties when I was born — and spin me yarns of my namesake king, and of Samuel and John the Baptist, other late-born sons who became servants of Jehovah. When I grew older, she told tales of my clan's history, which by her account so closely paralleled Genesis and Exodus that we might have been Children of Israel. The old lady knew how to tell a story; later, when I read the Scripture for myself, I would realize she was not above altering the timing of even a biblical tale to add suspense and surprise. In her revised standard version, David knocked out Goliath with his fifth stone, not his first, and the Philistine staggered around for half an hour before finally falling to the ground.

In addition to action, Grandmother's stories had authority, for though my clan was partrilineal, patrilocal, and prima facie male-dominated, it was in fact a matriarchy. My father may have been High Priest, my Uncle John Chieftain, but Grandmother was Judge, as in Israelite tradition. When I was born she had held office for over half a century, and her influence extended into every aspect of my life, even to my play.

Grandmother did not hold with play. While recreation *might* enable one to work with renewed vigor, play was linked with acts unholy, for it was written in Exodus, chapter 32, that after defiling their spirits by worshiping the golden calf, the Children of Israel "rose up to play." She accepted that children needed play, and that I, entirely deprived of it, might become the proverbial dull boy. But she paid more heed to Proverbs, wherein was written, "Even a child is known by his doings, whether his work be pure, and whether it be right," and she taught me, quoting First Corinthians, that if I wanted to be a Christian, a man, and a minister, I had to put away such childish needs.

Verily, I would have despised her, had she not known that work and play are the same thing under differing conditions, and mastered the knack of making the former seem like the latter. As it was, I spent many a contented day at her place, my clan's Homestead, a clapboard-faced log farmhouse equipped with neither central heat nor running water, helping her stack wood, split kindling, or fetch water from the spring that welled up cold and pure in a shady glen a hundred yards away. Such tasks were becoming outmoded, even in the rural mountain coutry where we lived; Grandmother used this increasing obsolescence to make them seem like frontier adventures.

When work was unmistakably that — even a dull boy cannot confuse liming the outhouse with having a good time — she'd enliven drudgery with more of her tales, these from the old days, when the workday stretched from can to can't and life was so routine that repainting the privy was almost a privilege.

Finally, when enough work had been done — you could never *finish* work, any more than you could finish the Bible — or in the evenings, after she, leaving the Homestead, came to my father's modern house, where she condescended to spend the night, she *might* find it permissible to play a game, but only because completely idle hands were Satan's workshop.

Still, Satan was the source of games — see Job, chapter 1. So Grandmother had a hierarchy of which games were less corrupting. She actually approved of checkers, and was herself adept at several varieties, especially Chinese. Of field games she was grudgingly accepting; young people had excessive energies, which, if not expended in work, were better exhausted outdoors in daylight than left undissipated indoors after dark. Of board games like Parcheesi, however, she entirely disapproved, for these games called for throwing at least one die, and sometimes dice. This led to more perditive pastimes; after all, the Romans had cast lots for Jesus' robes. As for card games — don't even mention them. In fact, don't mention cards, for they in themselves were evil. What could you do with cards but gamble? And what were the depictions of kings, queens, and jacks but violations of the Second Commandment, at least in spirit? No deck of cards had ever crossed the threshold of the Homestead, nor were such allowed in my father's house; when my mother once introduced an Old Maids deck, Grandmother threw it in the stove, lest I learn to shuffle.

This made sense to me, not only because I revered Grandmother (though sometimes I didn't like her much) but also because, when I had seen cards played in television Westerns, they were associated with smoking and drinking and led inevitably to fights. Though I was sometimes tempted by other sins, I did not find card games intriguing; I had sampled both tobacco and Demon Rum when the chance was offered by some of my less holy cousins (on my mother's side, of course), but when they'd offered to teach me pinochle I hotly refused. Now, at almost ten, though I sometimes touched myself, I had never touched a card. But here was my mother, suggesting a card game — and on the Sabbath! She would never have done such a thing had Grandmother been there. But Grandmother wasn't there. She was dead. I had killed her.

I hadn't meant to kill her. I had just wanted to reconcile the Gospel of Matthew — wherein Jesus commanded, among other things, "Love your enemies, bless them that curse you, do good to them that hate you, and pray for them which despitefully use you, and persecute you" — with the fact that I was being bullied and beaten up on the school playground with appalling regularity and sometimes dangerous severity. This was hard spiritual teaching, but my pastoral destiny demanded that I try to follow it, and I was doing fairly well. But I was doing less well with other parts of the Gospel. Like "resist not evil: but whosoever shall smite thee on thy right cheek, turn to him the other also," and the required attitudes in the Beatitudes. I didn't see, for example, how I could be a peacemaker when I was not making the war, or how I could feel blessed for being meek when by the time I inherited the earth, I'd be six feet under it, or how I could rejoice and be exceedingly glad about being reviled and persecuted when my reward would be in Heaven. I wanted to go to Heaven, of course, but not quite yet.

My training had not equipped me to grapple with such questions. My training had not equipped me to grapple with *any* questions of a spiritual nature. Certainly I had not been taught to ask questions; if questions somehow arose, I was supposed to search for answers in Scripture. Right was following the Commandments — see Exodus — or the teachings of Jesus — see the Gospels, or the Epistles, or Acts. Wrong was forgetting of the Covenant or of the Lord — see Deuteronmy. Pain was testing — see Job. Though I had been allowed, even encouraged, to explore the physical world without restraint, when it came to the metaphysical world I had been given a road map and instructions from Isaiah: "This is the Way, walk ye in it." My clan's tradition was exegetical, not charismatic; I'd been taught to heed not ranting exhortations or parroted precepts, but well-worded meditations and clear positions supported by citations from the Bible. But I had not been taught to test meditation against observation, nor to extrapolate static position into dynamic action, nor even to compare one Scripture with another; rather, I had been taught to overlook inconsistencies, rationalize apparent contradictions. And I had learned well; I could cite passages, behave kindly and gently, just as I could do simple calculations: add, subtract, multiply, divide, even use a slide rule. But there were branches of human mathematics I did not even know existed — the geometry of history, the algebra of hate and fear and prejudice, the calculus of irony.

And so, predictably, when I tried to plot a human vector on a religious graph I failed, and committed serious sins. First, an act of violence — a clear violation of the Beatitudes, and but for the grace of God, the Sixth Commandment. Then, a failure to repent; what I well knew was wrong felt justified, necessary and *right*. Then, a thought; that what felt right *was* right — that Faith, the Gospel, the Teaching of Jesus, was really what was wrong.

As soon as that thought came to me, I knew my life was over. For though I did not know the word "heresy," I knew for a true Christian such a thought would have been unthinkable. I knew God would forgive me for thinking it, if I could truly and earnestly repent, but I could not imagine He would ever after Call me to His ministry. I was certain I had lost my destiny, and worse, my family's destiny — single-handedly, I had blown a century-and-a-quarter-long tradition. Nor was I going to be able to keep it secret; although it was not absolutely necessary that I receive my Call soon, it had been known to happen to some as young as I. I had always been precocious. Surely I had never been slow. So sooner or later, I was going to have to explain why I, unlike my fathers before me, was not acceptable to God, and the later it got the more explaining I would have to do. Either that, or I was going to have to fake the Call — which notion only proved how far I'd fallen and pushed me further from Grace.

For months I wrestled with the problem. Finally I decided my only course was to preempt Jehovah: to publicly exchange what was no longer my sacred destiny for something that might get me back into the Grace of God — and off the hook with Man. I would, I decided, become a scientist — a doctor or a physicist. Instead of battling Satan directly, I would wrestle with pestilence or famine or war. I'd find a cure for something, like Jonas Salk, or a zillion uses for something humble, like George Washington Carver, or a way to keep the Russian H-bomb from exploding.

So through the spring and summer of 1959 I practiced diligently with my Acu-math slide rule, spent hours doing experiments with my Gilbert microscope and chemistry sets. To the disconcertion of the county librarian, I abandoned fictional "storybooks" in favor of factual texts; by the time school resumed, I had fought my way through *Kon-Tiki* and *Deliver Us from Evil*, and had so thoroughly absorbed the Real Book series that I could discourse *extempore* and *ad nauseam* on such topics as "The Submarine from David Bushnell's *Turtle* to the USS *Nautilus*" or "The Indian Tribes of North America." Then, toward the end of September, a few weeks after my ninth birthday, I happened on what seemed a way to mitigate my failure. One chill October afternoon I informed Grandmother that when I grew up I wanted to be a medical missionary, like Albert Schweitzer or Tom Dooley. I did not have the courage to make it explicit, but the implication was clear: I did not intend to preach.

Grandmother said nothing, then or ever. For weeks I wondered if she accepted my new vocation or was just waiting on the Lord to change my mind. But when, in early December, she went into physical decline, I could not help but think that she was sick with disappointment. When she died, just after Christmas, I believed I'd killed her, never mind that she was ninety-one. Following her funeral, I dedicated myself to regaining my lost destiny. I cleaved unto Grandmother's teachings more faithfully than when she was alive, and sought more rules to follow; I parsed the Pentateuch like some pedomorphic Essenian, and forced myself to accept as necessary whatever I read there.

Though my behavior was motivated mostly by guilt, terror was also a factor. My mother, seeing that I shied away from Grandmother's body laid out in the funeral home, had told me Grandmother was not really there, but in Heaven, watching over me. My mother meant well but failed to realize how literal were my notions of the Afterlife. Hell — a cave of horror where there was fire and brimstone always and forever, ruled by red devils and a snaky, scaly monster — was *real* to me. No less real was Heaven, where All God's (Departed) Children were issued white robes and shoes, haloes, and wings, and given power to look down upon the earth. The idea that Grandmother was there did not make me feel watched over; it made me feel *watched*. Alive, the old lady had been able to suspect, sometimes anticipate, my mischiefs; now she didn't have to think, all she had to do was look. There had to be some limit on what she could see, for the penalty for what I sometimes did beneath my sheets was to be struck dead — see Genesis 38:9–10. Of course, it was the Lord who slew Onan, but I did not fear God half so much as I feared Grandmother. Which was why I quaked in my hightops when my mother asked me to leave Leviticus and play cards on Sunday.

Since, I have sometimes wondered at my mother's motivation. Perhaps she hoped to shock me out of what was obviously an unhealthy state of mind. Perhaps she had merely tired of my being a pietistic pain in the posterior. Or perhaps she had a vision of the Afterlife as literal as I, pictured Grandmother looking down from Paradise, and wanted to blow the fuses in the old lady's halo; though of course I didn't realize it, Grandmother and my mother had cordially despised each other for decades.

I have also sometimes wondered if my mother knew she was at risk. For in my aberrant state of mind I might have been capable of rejecting her as an Agent of Satan, tempting me with pasteboard iniquity. Fortunately I had been steeped in the Principle of Obedience. Though I had not been trained to be a "good Nazi" — indeed, I was told that even though I was a child, I was solely responsible for my acts — I had been taught that personal understanding was not requisite for right action and that it was more important that I follow instructions than that I know the reason for them. In fact, I believed I had no right to reasons, or to think that any offered would seem reasonable to me. Though I did not love Obedience, I did not question it, for examples of it were all around me. Daily I saw my Elders striving to obey the Word of God, despite the illogic and injustice of His world. I saw them praying prayers that were not answered clearly, if at all, and persevering in the face of pain, insult, indignity. I believed I too had to learn to act on faith, and if I did not have faith, to act as if I did. In the meantime there was the Commandment to obey, which put it simply: Honor thy father and mother.

So when my mother asked me not just to touch a playing card but to take an *entire deck* into my hand, I did so — but only because the cards were still in the box. Then she told me to open the box, and I found myself between the Scylla of immorality and the Charybdis of disobedience. But in that strait I found insight, and opportunity; this, I decided, was one of those moments when I had to act on faith. I whispered a prayer, closed my eyes, and removed the first card from the box.

Nothing happened.

After a minute I opened my eyes and saw why there had been neither earthquake nor lightning bolt: this card was different from any of the cards over which men died in Dodge City or Tombstone Territory. Although it displayed the black, satanic symbol that denoted the ace of spades, it also bore a human face.

It was not a good face. Nor was it a bad one. It was too . . . complicated for such words. The hair was an unruly white mane, echoed by a fulsome, unabashed mustache; this suggested the rebellious, or worse, the libertine. But the brow was furrowed, as if in disapproval; the nose, presented in left half-profile, was aquiline, authoritative; the jaw was unyielding, the chin severe. And the eyes — there was something *sinister* about the eyes; the left one seemed fixed on some object in the middle distance, the right one peered out accusingly from behind the high nasal bridge.

Few children would have found this portrait prepossessing. But I found it eased my soul. For I recognized it as the visage of an Elder — craggy, experienced, and stern. This, I realized, not the countenance cosmetologically imposed upon her by a saccharine mortician, was the true expression of Grandmother's life and teaching. Seeing it on this playing card, I understood that I loved the old lady far more than I feared her, and missed her more than I could ever say.

And so I came to play cards on Sunday. The game was called Authors, a literary variation on that venerable children's pastime Go Fish. I'd never played Go Fish and never would — but I did play Authors, in which the usual denominations were assigned to some famous writer, with each card in that denomination representing one of that writer's works and each of the four aces was a novel by Mark Twain. In the coming weeks and months I continued to play Authors, and with a conscience that was almost clear, for I rationalized that these were not really *cards* but *books*, something of which Grandmother had heartily approved.

And if ascent to heaven had gifted her with an enlarged perspective, Grandmother approved my playing, because Authors was for me a vital canon, introducing me by name to some of the great writers and texts. I lost my innocence of cards, but I also lost my ignorance of literature. In the next few years the game would guide me to read works that even my most encouraging mentors might have said were inappropriate to my age. I took a run at *Julius Caesar* and delighted in the language, which reminded me of the King James Bible, though I had no real understanding of what was ultimately at issue. I was less delighted with *The Deerslayer* — I hated Cooper's prose, found his woodcraft ludicrous and his Indians lacking in the spiritual life other reading had taught me to expect — but I liked Longfellow and was excited by the rhythm of "Song of Hiawatha." Though I did not know a trochee from an anapest, I identified with the characters and situation of Whittier's "Snow-Bound." By the time I started junior high I had at least attempted many of the works everybody wants to have read and nobody wants to read. But none would mean as much to me as the works from the Authors canon that I first took up: two novels by Mark Twain.

I was a few days shy of six years old when I first saw the face of bigotry. It was September of 1956. I was on the playground, during the first recess of my first day of school, looking to make friends, as my mother said I should. I approached a little boy of Irish ancestry. Shyly, I introduced myself. The little Irish boy took one look at me and called me a nigger.

This was more or less predictable, for though I did not grow up in a locale renowned for racial outrage, in the outback of Arkansas or Alabama, say, or of Mississippi or Missouri, I did grow up in the mountains of western

Pennsylvania, an area with some history of hostility — in the 1920s the Klan had been a major political party — and the kind of rural isolation some find picturesque, idyllic, even virtuous.

In 1956, the poor little one-horse town outside of which I lived, though it was the largest for forty miles and the county seat, had three traffic lights, one thousand-watt sunup-to-sundown AM radio station, and a telephone system entirely dependent on human operators. Locals thought of the place as God's Country, in part because there were a hundred and seventy-three churches there, by actual count. But if it was God's Country, He had no love of blacks. In 1910, when my clan immigrated, there was a Negro community of perhaps four score and ten, but by 1960 there were only a third as many blacks as churches, and in terms of racial brotherhood it was a valley in the shadow of nowhere.

Not that the whites were bigots, exactly. But many lived in secluded coves and hollows, in a rustic style about which only an opiated romantic would rhapsodize; a sober realist would have termed their lives depressing, delimiting, and deprived. Many of these whites had never left the county; some had seldom been to town. To them, Negroes were *rarae aves*, as unusual as such miracles of rare device as radio, telephone, and indoor plumbing; their feelings may have been hostile but were as much xenophobic as racist.

Some of their more cosmopolitan cousins were real racists, classic ones, who justified white political supremacy on a theory of white superiority taken from Scripture: Negroes wore the mark of Cain or were the accursed sons of Ham. But most whites, if asked, would have paid at least lip service to brotherhood; more than a few preached it, and some practiced what they preached. Still, even most of these were segregationists who believed that "folks should stick to their own kind."

And so God's Country had a number of quaint customs reminiscent of points south of Mason and Dixon's Line. No law, and few formal customs, mandated segregation, but basically blacks lived, loved, worshiped God, died, and were buried among themselves; and in all things purely social they were separate as the thumb.

This made God's Country seem a placid place, for that which was not *de jure*, or even uniformly *de facto*, could be kept *sub rosa*. Blacks who did not like it left it; those who stayed stayed quiet, in part because their heads were in the lion's mouth, in part because they *liked* quiet. Though there were incidents from time to time, confrontations were short-lived and physical assaults virtually unknown.

Verbal disparagements were, if not unheard of, then unheard. Some blacks spoke resentfully of whites, but never said a mumbling word when any whites were present. Whites were equally circumspect. Though few used the term "Negro," which my family preferred, most blacks were not insulted by the term most whites did use: "colored." Even bigots did not say "nigger" to a black person's face; in God's Country, all but the worst bigots were polite.

But "nigger" did come trippingly off some white tongues when no blacks were present. Somehow children learned the word. Even if they had been bred in some hillbilly hollow where a black child was a vague abstraction, they knew one when they saw one, and what to call him when they did. So it was with the little boy of Irish ancestry, whose dress and accent suggested that the school bus had transported him to what must have seemed to him an alien place. No doubt he felt lost, and terrified — terrified, perhaps, of me. But before he boarded that bus he'd learned the word "nigger," and that someone who looked like me should be hurt by it.

I had learned no such thing. Though my Elders had wanted to warn me about "nigger" and the iceberg of bigotry of which it was the tip, my mother had insisted I not be led to expect an evil I might not experience. Until the little boy of Irish ancestry hurled his epithet, I had never heard the word. I had never even heard *of* it. I did not know what a nigger was, or that I was supposed to be one, or that hearing the word was supposed to hurt me. So I stood there, unintimidated, uncomprehending, certainly uninjured, albeit a bit confused. Which confused him. He grew impatient, then frustrated — his face turned pink, then red. "Nigger!" he repeated, shouting, as if he thought I might be deaf. Then he punched me in the nose.

Such things did not happen every day, but they were fairly frequent — more frequent as I acquired a reputation for being good at schoolwork. They did not always escalate from insult to assault, but it happened often enough to make insults alone terrifying. I still did not know what "nigger" meant, but I began to cringe before the word, as if I had been struck. I made no mention of this persecution; the bruises did not show much on my brown skin; the stains I explained away as residue of spontaneous nosebleeds.

But eventually my Elders discovered what was going on. My mother, who at the time had lived in God's Country for less than a decade, swore to put a stop to it, and telephoned some of the other mothers. She learned a lesson about God's Country when one of them called *her* a nigger. Grandmother, who had resided in God's Country for almost half a century, said I might as well learn now how to deal with "poor white trash," and taught me to keep my expression impassive and move past my tormentors sedately, or turn and walk away "with dignity" — all in order to deny the poor white trash the satisfaction of knowing they had hurt my feelings. My father, who had grown up in God's Country, said I should learn to *have* no feelings; then sticks and stones might break my bones, but names would never hurt me.

It seemed my father missed the fact that these little bigots were *using* sticks and stones, but I accepted his instruction, and Grandmother's, and worked to master my new lessons. Meanwhile, I happened on a technique of my own: to retaliate with nastier names. Grandmother had unknowingly supplied one basic formulation, and by attending to the vernacular of some of the less pious blacks in town, I compiled a lexicon of racial insults. I understood the connotation of "trash," "redneck," "peckerwood," or "ofay" no better than I understood that of "nigger," but I wielded those words with force and flair, and soon I learned to modify the nouns with vulgar adjectives. Usually this language set the little bigots back on their heels long enough for me to walk away with what looked like dignity — though in my heart I knew I was running scared.

In September of 1958, when I was almost eight, verbal retaliation began to fail. Frank exchanges of epithets led to violent attacks with greater frequency. From these I could not defend myself, for I lacked both the training and the will to fight. I had been taught that physical resistance was morally wrong. So I did what I had been trained to do: I took it to the Lord in prayer. I thought I'd found a surefire formula in the language of Psalm 144, and while winter kept us much indoors, it did seem God had promised to "rid me, and deliver me from the hand of strange children."

But that spring, on Good Friday, as it happened, God failed to protect me. In protecting myself I committed the violent act that led to heresy and the loss of my destiny, and my clan's. Though I longed for redemption, I clung to the fruit of heresy: a clear decision to defend myself by any means necessary. Even after Grandmother's death and my rededication to the faith, I continued to do battle, for the way of meekness seemed a sure road to suicide. But though I fought, I understood I could not win. Violence was *wrong*; therefore victory was no reason for rejoicing ; indeed, every triumph took me further from salvation, and made it less likely I could regain my destiny. Yet it seemed that the only way to preserve my body was to put my soul in peril.

In fact, my mind was in greater peril. For though I still did not know many of the connotations of the word "nigger," I had come to a fuller understanding of the phrase "poor white trash." At first I had assumed white trash identified themselves as such by the way they treated me, but eventually I noticed that the children most prone to insult and assault me did tend to be poor. They also tended to come from families which were less educated, less sober, less hardworking, less devout than mine. Though I had thought little about "poor white trash" while Grandmother was alive, after her death, like all her recollected utterances, it assumed biblical proportions. I began to see whites who were poor as both enemies and social and intellectual inferiors. And so, despite my suffering at the hands of bigots, by August of 1960, I was well on the way to becoming a bigot myself.

Enter, to the rescue, the Authors ace of spades, *The Adventures of Tom Sawyer*, which I borrowed from the county library, much to the relief of the librarian, who found my penchant for nonfiction abnormal. But in fact I checked the novel out because "the author" assured me that it *wasn't* fiction, but rather a recording of "adventures" that had "really occurred," and that the people who appeared in it were real — Tom Sawyer was a combination of three boys, but somebody else named Huck Finn was "drawn from life."

And indeed, when I read in the opening lines how Aunt Polly "pulled her spectacles down and looked over them" and then "put them up and looked out under them," I felt a warm surge of recognition and affection, for I had seen Grandmother do those very things at least a thousand times. I also liked Sid, the "quiet boy" with "no adventurous, troublesome ways," who attended school regularly, and liked it, and always did his chores; he reminded me of me. And I was thoroughly intrigued by "the small colored boy," the hardworking Jim, who was the first Negro I had ever seen in a storybook. I did not realize Jim was a slave and had no choice other than to be industrious; I just noted that even when Tom supposedly helped Jim split kindling, "Jim did three-fourths of the work," and I liked Jim the more because of it.

I did not like Tom. He was a lazy, lying hooky-player, and not so much clever as slick. My dislike crystallized at the end of the first chapter, where Tom picks a fight with a boy who is better dressed and a stranger. Though the insults that lead to combat are nonracial, I read my experience and myself into the situation. While I did not see this strange boy as black, I did see him as *me*, assaulted for no reason other than difference. Tom, I decided, had he lived in God's Country, would have been among the worst of my tormentors.

So disgusted was I with Tom that I almost put the book down at the end of chapter 1. But I had learned from hours of Bible reading to peruse with patience and persistence, and so pushed on to chapter 2. Then things grew complicated. Jim made his second appearance, and I saw that he was a slave, and worse, that he had to kowtow to "Marse Tom," and worst, that Aunt Polly, who seemed so much like Grandmother, owned him.

Again I almost put the book down. Once more I persisted, and was rewarded with rich recountings of the familiar rituals of Sunday services, and with a scene of poetic punishment for Tom, who not only broke Commandments, but failed to take learning Scriptures seriously, and even perverted Sunday school to accomplish selfish ends.

At that point I thought I understood what the story was about: sin and salvation. Obviously, these characters were going to see the error of their ways. Aunt Polly was already crying over a minor wrong done to Tom; she would soon see she was doing a major wrong to Jim. And Tom would either repent or come to a gruesome end. I read on, at least half hoping for the latter resolution. But then another character entered, and upset my simplistic morality play.

I hated Huck as soon as I saw him, for he seemed to epitomize the poor white trash that was making my life miserable. But then I began to pity him. Unlike Tom, I did not envy Huck the "freedom" to sleep "on doorsteps in fine weather and in empty hogsheads in wet." I didn't know what a hogshead was, but it sounded like it had something to do with pigs. I knew pigs, and so I saw nothing romantic in Huck's sleeping arrangements, or in any other aspect of his poverty, illiteracy, and religious sciolism. Indeed, Huck seemed lonely and sad. I fixed on his status as "the juvenile pariah of the village," whose society was forbidden to other boys, whose condition was outcast. Not that I saw myself in him, but I did know how he must have felt. Sympathy became empathy, and a subconscious decision to give Huck a chance. After all, he hadn't done anything bad . . . and then he did, in one bit of dialogue, concerning the use of "spunk-water" to cure warts: "Jeff told Johnny Baker, and Johnny told Jim Hollis, and Jim told Ben Rogers, and Ben told a nigger, and the nigger told me."

That did it for Huckleberry Finn, that ignorant redneck white trash peckerwood. That did it for Tom Sawyer, too, because he replied, "They'll all lie. Leastways all but the nigger. I don't know *him*. But I never see a nigger that *wouldn't* lie." In fact that did it for the book; that book was *closed*. Had it not been property of the county library, that book would have suffered serious damage.

But what was so easily put out of sight was not so easily put out of mind, for when my fury faded it came to me that what went on in the book was actually quite similar to what happened in God's Country. The author, this Mark Twain, was like the white people who were not bigots. He called Negroes "negroes," or "colored," which was acceptable. He did use the word "nigger," but only to report what the people in the book said — people he'd grown up with, "schoolmates of mine," he'd written. In that sense, I used "nigger" too — how else would I describe what the little bigots called me? And even Huck and Tom, although they used the word, did not use it in front of Jim. Nor did they beat him up. So I went back to the book.

Then I realized something more complicated: both Huck and Tom used the word, but with a crucial difference. When Huck said "nigger" he meant somebody who was a Negro but as truthful as a person who was white. Tom rejected the Negro's knowledge, and not because he'd known this Negro to lie; Tom knew nothing about the Negro, not even his name. When Tom said "nigger" he meant somebody who was a liar because he was a Negro, and for no other reason. Tom Sawyer was a bigot. But Huck accepted the knowledge of this Negro — this *nigger*. He set the nigger equal with the white boys, and apparently thought nothing of it.

Once again I found myself sympathizing with Huck, making excuses for him. Tom was supposedly a respectable boy, with the advantages of education and religion; for him to use the word "nigger" was obviously wrong. But Huck was ignorant, innocent of both public and Sunday school. Perhaps he knew no better than to say "nigger." I found myself actually liking him, and when I went back to the book it was not to follow the adventures of Tom Sawyer but to discover the fate of Huckleberry Finn. I was overjoyed that in the end he was rescued from poverty, homelessness, illiteracy, and apostasy — that he slept on clean sheets, went to school, was taught the Bible; that he had a future on earth and a chance at Heaven. Since I knew from the Authors cards that there was a book by the name of *Adventures of Huckleberry Finn*, that was the next thing I borrowed from the library.

I did not know that *Huckleberry Finn* was a trickier text than *Tom Sawyer*. I did not know that dramatic irony and first-person narration created serious critical problems, or that subtleties of grammar and diction — like the difference between connotation and denotation — were beyond my intellectual grasp. I did not even realize I was reading fiction — how could I, when in the conclusion of *Tom Sawyer*, Twain claimed not only that the characters were real, but that most of them still lived? And so Huck lived for me, though I felt a bit superior to him, since I already knew how to read and had long understood that Moses had been dead a considerable time. And I understood that the word "nigger" appeared often because Huck was doing the writing, as well as much of the talking. I was a bit surprised to find that Jim used it — I had never imagined a Negro would use that word, much less heard one do so — but I was so happy to see him again that I let it slide; such was my unsophistication that I thought this was Jim from *Tom Sawyer* miraculously grown to manhood.

Eventually I forgave Huck's use of the word, for I noticed that while he occasionally referred to Jim as a nigger, he never *called* him nigger. The difference was clear when Huck's father used the word, railing about "a prowling, thieving, infernal, white-shirted free nigger" who was also a college professor. Pap Finn's use of "nigger" was not only insulting but indiscriminate; he hated Negroes, even if they were as clean and respectable as any Negro could be; Huck, for all his crudeness, was obviously better than his upbringing. This impressed me.

What impressed me more, as I read on, was not what Huck called Jim but the way he treated him. Tom wanted to tie Jim up, but Huck refused and wouldn't even go with Tom when he crawled off to play a trick on Jim. Huck would not tell Judge Thatcher that he feared his father had returned, but he did tell Jim. And though in *Tom Sawyer*, Huck says eating with a Negro is something "a body's got to do . . . when he's awful hungry" that "he wouldn't want to do as a steady thing," in his own book Huck just says to Jim, "Pass me along another hunk of fish and some hot corn-bread."

I was still more impressed by what happens on the one occasion when Huck is unkind to Jim. After being lost in thick fog, he plays a Sawyerish trick on Jim and calls him "a tangle-headed old fool." Jim fights back with word I recognized: "Dat truck dah is *trash*; en trash is what people is dat puts dirt on de head er dey fren's en makes 'em ashamed." Though I could not then appreciate the risk Jim ran by showing such spirit to a white, I recognized the virtue in Huck's response.

> It was fifteen minutes before I could work myself up to go and humble myself to a nigger — but I done it, and I warn't ever sorry for it afterward, neither.

But what most impressed me — what almost had to, given my upbringing — was the moment in chapter 31 when Huck resolves that rather than turn Jim in he'll go to Hell. Not that I thought that Huck was really wrong. But I understood that Huck thought he was wrong, and thought he would go to a Hell as literal as the one in which I myself believed. I was awed by Huck's defiance. I *admired* it. I wondered if I would have the courage to do such a thing. I wondered if St. John might not have quoted Jesus incorrectly, for it was clear to me that to lay down your soul for a friend required greater love than to lay down your life.

I did not think much more about Mark Twain for almost a decade. During that time I did not become a literary sophisticate; though I read a number of the classics, I also devoured a lot of so-called trash, and often got the categories mixed. (I thought *A Connecticut Yankee* had much in common with *Glory Road*, a science fantasy penned by Twain's fellow Missourian Robert A. Heinlein.) But at least I learned what fiction *was*, and how to deal with symbolism and several types of irony.

I did become what some might call a religious sophisticate — or a secular humanist. Not that I became an atheist, but I stopped believing in a literal Hell or a factual Bible, or that the solution to every earthly problem could be found in Scripture. Rather, I decided the solution to every earthly problem could be found in a library, provided it had books enough.

Certainly that seemed true for me. It was not hyperbole to say that books borrowed from the county library had kept me almost sane during my adolescence in God's Country. And when, in the fall of 1968, I matriculated at the University of Pennsylvania in Philadelphia, I quickly found refuge from the cultural contradictions thrust upon me by the City of Brotherly Love and the Ivy League in the Van Pelt Library. Partly to escape the dormitory and my ultra-preppy roommate, I studied there almost every night, and when I wasn't doing assignments, I went roaming through the stacks, picking books at random. I had been admitted to the university's General Honors Program, and one of the perks was access to a private study lounge, where I could stretch out on a couch, drink a smuggled-in cup of coffee, and think in peace. It was there that I learned to *read* — not just to absorb a text, but to trace origins, parse meanings. It was there that I discovered the power of plain language. And it was there, at long last, that I received my Call — not to minister, but to write.

This was not the usual undergraduate "career decision"; that, I'd already made. I was as serious about writing as a student could be. I took creative writing workshops, invented my own major so I could take more writing courses, submitted stories to campus magazines, even collected rejection slips from all the best national magazines and journals. But though I hoped I'd make a living as a writer, I had never seen that as a replacement for the ministry. Then one night I underwent a classic conversion experience, with symptoms right out of William James — heart palpitations, euphoria, a sensation of mental clarity. I felt that some internal void had suddenly been filled, that I knew, now, not what I wanted to do in life, but what I was *supposed* to do. I felt free and happy and ineffably light.

It was a glorious moment, but it fell somewhat short of Pentecost — the Spirit filled me but somehow failed to give me the gift of utterance; no multitudes gathered suddenly to marvel at my words. My fellow students still had trouble understanding my characters' motivations. My teachers were neither more encouraging nor less critical — those who heard me bear witness to my experience suspected I was full of new wine. Meanwhile, editors who weighed my work in the balance still found it wanting.

Had I been trained in a more demonstrative tradition I might have been discouraged. But I knew that even in matters of faith, spirit alone was insufficient; you might have been licked by tongues as of fire, but you still had to go to seminary. I was already at a university — a secular seminary — and I thought all I had to do was follow the formula of the curriculum: read the work of great writers, and write constantly, sometimes in imitation of those writers, until I "found my own voice," as they say. It might even have been that simple had I not been black and had it not been the fag end of the sixties. But I was and it was, and so I was forced to deal with a host of complications arising out of something called "The Black Aesthetic."

The assumption behind the Black Aesthetic was that there was or ought to be some *difference* between works of art produced by persons of African ancestry, black Americans in particular, and those produced by persons of European ancestry, white Americans in particular. The idea had its origins in the eighteenth-century European belief that there were inherent physical, intellectual, and even moral differences between the races (with the Europeans being superior, of course), which could be measured by the standard of literary production — by the fact, as one Frenchman put it, that "Negroes . . . have never written a philosophical treatise, and never will." This notion was promoted in America by Thomas Jefferson, who reported in his *Notes on the State of Virginia*,

> . . . never yet could I find that a black had uttered a thought above the level of a plain narration. . . . Misery is often the parent of the most affecting touches in poetry. — Among the blacks is misery enough, God knows, but no poetry. Love is the peculiar cestrum of the poet. Their love is ardent, but it kindles the senses only, not the imagination.

Jefferson used this literary "evidence" to argue that blacks "are inferior to the whites in the endowments both of body and mind," and that this "unfortunate difference . . . of faculty, is a powerful obstacle to the emancipation of these people."

For the next hundred and fifty years or so, Negro intellectuals wasted their time trying to argue the reverse. As late as 1931, for example, James Weldon Johnson declared:

> The world does not know that a people is great until that people produces great literature and art. No people that has produced great literature and art has ever been looked on by the world as distinctly inferior. The status of the Negro in the United States is more a question of national attitude toward the race than of actual conditions. And nothing will do more to change that mental attitude and raise his status than a demonstration of intellectual parity by the Negro through the production of literature and art.

But a few years later, in his "Blueprint for Negro Writing," Richard Wright dismissed most "Negro writing in the past" as a collection of "prim and decorous ambassadors who went a-begging to white America . . . dressed in the

knee-pants of servility, curtsying to show that the Negro was not inferior";
and by the fifties and sixties many black intellectuals had more or less agreed
that consciously attempting to demonstrate anything to white people through
literature was both counterproductive and counterrevolutionary. LeRoi
Jones, even before he took the name Baraka, claimed there in fact *was* no legitimate Negro literature, nor had there ever been, because historically
"Negroes who found themselves in a position to pursue some art, especially
the art of literature, have been members of the Negro middle class."

Oddly, ironically, perhaps even embarrassingly, Jones sometimes agreed
with Jefferson. Of pioneer black poet Phillis Wheatley — he called her
"Phillis Whatley" — Jefferson said, "The compositions published under her
name are below the dignity of criticism." Jones said that Wheatley's "pleasant
imitations of eighteenth century English poetry are . . . ludicrous departures
from the huge black voices that splintered southern nights with their *hollers,
chants, arwhoolies, and ballits.*" If there was ever going to be a Negro literature, Jones went on to insist, "it must disengage itself from the weak, heinous
elements of the culture that spawned it," and learn that "the most successful
fiction of most Negro writing is in its emotional content."

Strong as Jones' opinion was, an even stronger one was in vogue in 1971,
especially among black students at the University of Pennsylvania. It was that
of James T. Stewart, a Philadelphia-based saxophonist whose essay "The
Development of the Black Revolutionary Artist" had been published in *Black
Dialogue* in the winter of 1966.

> The dilemma of the "negro" artist is that he makes assumptions based on
> the wrong models. He makes assumptions based on white models. These
> assumptions are not only wrong, they are even antithetical to his existence.
> The black artist must construct models which correspond to his own real-
> ity. The models must be non-white. Our models must be consistent with a
> black style, our natural aesthetic styles, and our moral and spiritual styles.

My dilemma was that I wanted — more, needed — to be an artist. Perforce,
I wanted to be a Negro artist, for it never occurred to me I *could* be any other
kind. But what Stewart called "white" models were the only ones I had — the

only ones I had ever had. From the point of view of the Black Aesthetic, I had spent my life reading all the wrong things — most recently, the texts required by the university's English department, before that, the Authors canon, and before that the hymns of Charles Wesley, Isaac Watts, and James Claire Taylor, and the King James Version of the Bible. In fact, these last were for me less models or assumptions than elements of my identity; I wasn't sure I could accept other models, even if I found them.

And finding them wasn't easy. Not that anthropological and archaeological descriptions of non-western art and culture, and even examples thereof, were entirely absent from the library's catalogue and stacks. But the essence of the argument was that nothing created by white people — which is to say, most of what was in the library, including the logic of the catalogue — could provide an accurate guide to the quality of the examples. As Stewart put it, "the point of the whole thing is that we must emancipate our minds from Western values and standards."

Which meant there was no reliable canon — not even the comfort of a card game. Nor did Jones or Stewart offer much help; they seemed to think the only American Negro art form worth talking about was music. Jones mentioned some writers — Jean Toomer, Richard Wright, Ralph Ellison, and James Baldwin — but only to damn them with faint praise.

Nor were there clear criteria by which a canon might be identified. It helped only somewhat to say that the texts should be "non-white" — which I assumed meant the author would be non-white. According to my own logic and the arguments of both Jones and Stewart, there had to be more to it. But what? Jones suggested that "Negro literature" should be "a legitimate prod-uct of the Negro experience in America," which suggested that the "more" might have something to do with another rubric then in vogue, the Black Experience. But that led to some nasty questions.

For example, though Phillis Wheatley's poetry was hardly "non-white" in form, Wheatley herself had been born in Africa and had lived there until she was seven or eight years old — long enough, surely, to have internalized some awareness of the cultural forms of her people. Then she had been captured, transported, auctioned, and enslaved; if there was a quintessential "Negro experience in America" Phillis Wheatley had it. So who was James T. Stewart, Philadelphia resident and player of an instrument invented in Paris, by a Frenchman, to suggest that her models were "antithetical?" Who was LeRoi Jones, born in Newark, educated at Howard, Columbia, and the New School for Social Research, to deride her as one who had failed to "tap" her "legitimate cultural tradition" and who "did not realize where the reality of [her] experience lay"? Maybe it was just that Wheatley, in her genius, discerned something Jones did not — a human, artistic, spiritual link between eighteenth-century English poetry and those "*hollers, chants, arwhoolies, and ballits.*"

Nor did it help to link "non-white" aesthetics to some political position. If, as Stewart said, "the point of the whole thing" was to "emancipate our minds," then surely one of my models had to be *Narrative of the Life of Frederick Douglass*, which was about mental and religious and spiritual liberation as much as physical liberation. True, Douglass had described how he derived the determination to resist whipping from a juju root provided by a "genuine African." But he'd also described how he derived artistic models from *The Columbian Orator*, how the documents it contained "gave tongue to interesting thoughts of my own soul, which had frequently flashed through my mind, and died away for want of utterance." Should Douglass have rejected Sheridan because he was not a Negro but an Irishman, and because the emancipation for which he called was not for Negroes but for Catholics? And should I reject the most powerful of the slave narratives because its formal antecedents were "white"?

And beyond the problem of the canon, there was the problem of aesthetic *principles* — the criteria by which something could be judged good or bad. Jones said, "A Negro literature, to be a legitimate product of the Negro experience in America, must get at that experience in exactly the terms America has proposed for it, in its most ruthless identity," but I couldn't make much sense of that, nor of "the most successful fiction of most Negro writing is in its emotional content"; maybe I was blind, or maybe it was the error of a white copyeditor, but it seemed to me that sentence didn't even track. And Stewart threw me for a total loop with this:

In our movement toward the future, "ineptitude" and "unfitness" will be an aspect of what we do. These are the words of the established order — the middle-class value judgments. We must turn these values on themselves . . . ultimately, be estranged from the dominant culture. This estrangement must be nurtured in order to generate and energize our black artists. This means that he cannot be "successful" in any sense that has meaning in white critical evaluations. Nor can his work ever be called "good" in any context or meaning that could make sense to that traditional critique.

Like every aspiring writer, I badly wanted to believe that all those who criticized my work were ignoramuses who could be ignored with impunity, and while I tried to tell myself that my artistic failures were in fact brilliant successes that suffered from being judged by Philistines according to inappropriate, European-oriented standards, I just could not accept an aesthetic theory that transformed me from apprentice to master craftsman without benefit of labor, especially a theory expressed in such reactive terms.

But if I did not accept it, or something like it, my fate, according to Jones, was to produce work of "agonizing mediocrity," especially as I was surely an embodiment of the Negro middle-class artist Jones had damned. And yet what Jones said about such artists was not true of me. I emphatically did *not* want to write only to "exhibit" my "familiarity with social graces," or look "at literature as merely another way of gaining prestige in the white world for the Negro middle-class." I emphatically *did* want to investigate the human soul. But I wanted to do it for what in Jones' view were emphatically the wrong reasons: moral imperatives drawn from precisely the models I was supposed to reject. It seemed I had to come up with something *different* — if I didn't, my work would be not only mediocre but almost sinful; like a minister who preached falsely, I would damn myself to the Hell in which I no longer — supposedly — believed.

For weeks I roamed the library stacks, looking for answers, finding none. But finally I came upon a fat volume with a thin title — *Literary Geniuses on Literary Genius*, or something like that. It was one of those hodgepodge anthologies slammed together in haste by academics desperate to pad the curriculum vitae, and published by presses too cheap to pay for permission to reprint anything protected by copyright. This particular academic had ranged widely through the public domain, coming up with everything from long-winded Greek expositions to whole sections from John Locke to pithy aphorisms from Chinese mystics and American humorists. One of those short statements caught my eye: "the difference between the *almost right* word and the *right* word is really a large matter — 'tis the difference between the lightning-bug and the lightning."

What attracted me was not that the attribution was to my old friend Mark Twain, but rather that there was nothing *cultural* about the statement. There was nothing political about it. There was nothing middle-class about it, nor anything black or white — except the meaning. There was nothing *linguistic* about it, either. Although in another language it might not be a bon mot, it would still make sense. It would make sense to an African; it would have to, because if it didn't, *Africans* couldn't make sense to other Africans. If you wanted to construct a literary aesthetic, it seemed like a pretty good place to start.

Of course, there was a problem: Mark Twain was a white guy. Worse, he was a middle- if not upper-class white guy. Worst, he was a Southerner. Stewart, Jones, et alia would have rejected him out of hand, and I almost did too. But fortunately that desperate academic had also included a longer piece called "How to Tell a Story," and fortunately I had not grown so narrow-minded as not to read it. That essay made it clear to me that Mark Twain understood the aesthetics of literature a lot better than Stewart or even Jones.

"How to Tell a Story" was premised on a frankly nationalistic aesthetic.

The humorous story is American, the comic story is English, the witty story is French . . .

 . . . The art of telling a humorous story . . . was created in America, and has remained at home.

But one was not able to tell an American story simply because one was an American — indeed, Twain began the essay with a careful disclaimer.

I do not claim that I can tell a story as it ought to be told. I only claim to know how a story ought to be told, for I have been almost daily in the company of the most expert story-tellers for many years.

Nor was one endowed with the ability to tell a humorous story by experience alone.

The humorous story is strictly a work of art — high and delicate art — and only an artist can tell it.

And then came the surprise: despite the opening disclaimer, at the end Twain talked about a story he himself told from the platform. He described it as a "negro ghost story," and proceeded to reproduce it in dialect. I knew that Jones and others would have called that cultural appropriation and derided it as an insult. But however Twain came by the tale, and however he told it, four things about his treatment of it could not be ignored. First, Twain had respect for the source of the tale and was not ashamed to acknowledge it — he specifically called the tale a "negro ghost story." Second, he had respect for the original form; the story was told in dialect, which meant that Twain, in telling it, took on a black persona — something he didn't seem to mind. Third, he had respect for the artistry of the form; far from implying that to tell a "negro ghost story" was an easy thing, he spoke of practicing the technique and said that getting the pause at the end right was "the most troublesome and aggravating and uncertain thing you ever undertook." To me, confused as I was about aesthetics in general, and the racial dynamics of aesthetics in particular, all this was tremendously exciting, for it seemed so clear, so . . . *settling*. Accordingly, I searched the stacks for other of Twain's aesthetic pronouncements.

I had to do a bit of digging, because those pronouncements were scattered about and often seemed offhand. One piece I happened upon was written, apparently, when an editor invited Twain to discourse on his methods. Twain claimed not to have any methods, but went on to give a different spin on the business of aesthetic models.

Let us guess that whenever we read a sentence and like it, we unconsciously store it away in our model-chamber; and it goes with the myriad of its fellows to the building, brick by brick, of the eventual edifice which we call our style. And let us guess that whenever we run across other forms — bricks — whose colour, or some other defect, offends us, we unconsciously reject these, and so one never finds them in our edifice. If I have subjected myself to any training processes, and no doubt I have, it must have been in this unconscious or half-conscious fashion. I think it unlikely that deliberate and consciously methodical training is usual in the craft. I think it likely that the training most in use is of this unconscious sort, and is guided and governed and made by-and-by unconsciously systematic, by an automatically-working taste — a taste which selects and rejects without asking you for any help, and patiently and steadily improves itself without troubling you to approve or applaud.

Of course I realized that Twain was begging the aesthetic question as much as answering it. From whence came the initial criteria by which bricks were accepted or rejected? And what of that line from the Gospel, "The stone which the builders rejected, the same is become the head of the corner"? And yet I was not so hung up on logic as to miss Twain's point: that whatever the aesthetic criteria were, and wherever they originated, the process of becoming a writer meant not applying them so much as internalizing them, and making them undeniably and idiosyncratically *yours*.

And unlike Jones and Stewart, Twain offered, in "Fenimore Cooper's Literary Offences," precise criteria. I was fascinated to discover that although his objections were not exactly what mine had been, he also rejected Cooper's Indians, and felt, as I had, that the book had been written by somebody who had never spent an hour in the woods. I did not at first realize that Twain was being his usual ironic self with all this business about the "nineteen rules governing literary art in the domain of romantic fiction," but by the time I figured out there was no such list outside Twain's own head, I had decided that the rules made *sense*. A tale *should* accomplish something and arrive somewhere; the episodes *should* be necessary parts of the tale; the characters *should* talk like normal people, and *should* be so clearly defined that the reader can predict their behavior. And even though I noticed that Twain only listed eighteen rules, it seemed to me they were a pretty good blueprint for writing — Negro writing included.

Of course Twain was still a white guy; his rules therefore constituted exactly the kind of "white model" that Stewart said a black artist had to eschew. Which left me with a problem until I found a little essay called "What Paul Bourget Thinks of Us," wherein was written:

> Does the native novelist try to generalize the nation? No, he lays plainly before you the ways and speech and life of a few people grouped in a certain place — his own place — and that is one book. In time he and his brethren will report to you the life and the people of the whole nation — the life of a group in a New England village; in a New York village; in a Texan village; in an Oregon village; in villages in fifty States and Territories; then the farm-life in fifty States and Territories; a hundred patches of life and groups of people in a dozen widely separated cities. And the Indians will be attended to; and the cowboys; and the gold and silver miners; and the negroes; and the Idiots and Congressmen; and the Irish, the Germans, the Italians, the Swedes, the French, the Chinamen, the Greasers; and the Catholics, the Methodists, the Presbyterians, the Congregationalists, the Baptists, the Spiritualists, the Mormons, the Shakers, the Quakers, the Jews, the Campbellites, the infidels, the Christian Scientists, the Mind-Curists, the Faith-Curists, the train-robbers, the White Caps, the Moonshiners. And when a thousand able novels have been written, *there* you have the soul of the people, the life of the people, the speech of the people; and not anywhere else can these be had. And the shadings of character, manners, feelings, ambitions, will be infinite. (188–89)

I sat there in the private lounge of the General Honors Program of the Van Pelt Library of the University of Pennsylvania, and I thought about that. I thought about being black and middle-class, and Christian — about all my antithetical models. I thought about James T. Stewart and all the black artists in the world, on the one hand, and Mark Twain on the other. I thought about

Grandmother. I thought about Aunt Polly. I thought about Jim, the runaway slave, who called himself rich because he had stolen himself, and about Huck, the piece of poor white trash, who first humbled himself to a nigger and then abandoned all hope of Heaven to free that nigger, and about the middle-class white Southern man who had created both of them. I thought not only about wanting and needing to write, but about what kind of writer I wanted to be, what kind of stories I wanted to tell. It seemed to me I had to decide, forever, between two things. I studied a minute, sort of holding my breath, and then I said to myself, "All right, then, I'll *go* to hell."

HOW TO TELL

A STORY

and Other Essays

HOW TO TELL A STORY
AND OTHER ESSAYS

MARK TWAIN

HOW TO TELL A STORY

AND OTHER ESSAYS

BY

MARK TWAIN

NEW YORK
HARPER & BROTHERS PUBLISHERS
1897

NOTE

"How to Tell a Story" originally appeared in *The Youth's Companion;* "In Defence of Harriet Shelley," "Fenimore Cooper's Literary Offences," "What Paul Bourget Thinks of Us," and 'The Private History of the 'Jumping Frog' Story," in the *North American Review;* "Travelling with a Reformer," in the *Cosmopolitan Magazine;* and "Mental Telegraphy Again," in *Harper's Magazine.* "A Little Note to Paul Bourget" has not before appeared in print in this country.

CONTENTS

HOW TO TELL A STORY

HOW TO TELL A STORY

The Humorous Story an American Development.—Its
Difference from Comic and Witty Stories.

I DO not claim that I can tell a story as it
ought to be told. I only claim to know how
a story ought to be told, for I have been almost daily in the company of the most expert
story-tellers for many years.

There are several kinds of stories, but only
one difficult kind—the humorous. I will talk
mainly about that one. The humorous story
is American, the comic story is English, the
witty story is French. The humorous story
depends for its effect upon the *manner* of the
telling; the comic story and the witty story
upon the *matter*.

The humorous story may be spun out to
great length, and may wander around as much
as it pleases, and arrive nowhere in particular; but the comic and witty stories must
be brief and end with a point. The humor-

ous story bubbles gently along, the others burst.

The humorous story is strictly a work of art—high and delicate art—and only an artist can tell it; but no art is necessary in telling the comic and the witty story; anybody can do it. The art of telling a humorous story— understand, I mean by word of mouth, not print — was created in America, and has remained at home.

The' humorous story is told gravely; the teller does his best to conceal the fact that he even dimly suspects that there is anything funny about it; but the teller of the comic story tells you beforehand that it is one of the funniest things he has ever heard, then tells it with eager delight, and is the first person to laugh when he gets through. And sometimes, if he has had good success, he is so glad and happy that he will repeat the "nub" of it and glance around from face to face, collecting applause, and then repeat it again. It is a pathetic thing to see.

Very often, of course, the rambling and disjointed humorous story finishes with a nub, point, snapper, or whatever you like to call it. Then the listener must be alert, for in many cases the teller will divert attention from that nub by dropping it in a carefully casual and indifferent way, with the pretence that he does not know it is a nub.

Artemus Ward used that trick a good deal; then when the belated audience presently caught the joke he would look up with innocent surprise, as if wondering what they had found to laugh at. Dan Setchell used it before him, Nye and Riley and others use it to-day.

But the teller of the comic story does not slur the nub; he shouts it at you—every time. And when he prints it, in England, France, Germany, and Italy, he italicizes it, puts some whooping exclamation-points after it, and sometimes explains it in a parenthesis. All of which is very depressing, and makes one want to renounce joking and lead a better life.

Let me set down an instance of the comic method, using an anecdote which has been popular all over the world for twelve or fifteen hundred years. The teller tells it in this way:

THE WOUNDED SOLDIER

In the course of a certain battle a soldier whose leg had been shot off appealed to another soldier who was hurrying by to carry him to the rear, informing him at the same time of the loss which he had sustained; whereupon the generous son of Mars, shouldering the unfortunate, proceeded to carry out his desire. The bullets and cannon-balls were flying in all directions, and presently one of the latter took the wounded man's head off— without, however, his deliverer being aware of it. In no long time he was hailed by an officer, who said:

"Where are you going with that carcass?"

"To the rear, sir—he's lost his leg!"

"His leg, forsooth?" responded the astonished officer; "you mean his head, you booby."

Whereupon the soldier dispossessed himself of his burden, and stood looking down upon it in great perplexity. At length he said:

"It is true, sir, just as you have said." Then after a pause he added, "*But he* TOLD *me* IT WAS HIS LEG!!!!!"

Here the narrator bursts into explosion after explosion of thunderous horse-laughter, repeating that nub from time to time through his gaspings and shriekings and suffocatings.

It takes only a minute and a half to tell that in its comic-story form; and isn't worth

the telling, after all.   Put into the humorous-
story form it takes ten minutes, and is about
the funniest thing I have ever listened to—as
James Whitcomb Riley tells it.

He tells it in the character of a dull-witted
old farmer who has just heard it for the first
time, thinks it is unspeakably funny, and is
trying to repeat it to a neighbor.   But he
can't remember it; so he gets all mixed up
and wanders helplessly round and round, putting in tedious details that don't belong in the
tale and only retard it; taking them out con-
scientiously and putting in others that are just
as useless; making minor mistakes now and
then and stopping to correct them and explain how he came to make them; remembering things which he forgot to put in in their
proper place and going back to put them in
there; stopping his narrative a good while in
order to try to recall the name of the soldier
that was hurt, and finally remembering that
the soldier's name was not mentioned, and remarking placidly that the name is of no real
importance, anyway — better, of course, if one
knew it, but not essential, after all—and so on,
and so on, and so on.

The teller is innocent and happy and pleased
with himself, and has to stop every little while

to hold himself in and keep from laughing out-
right; and does hold in, but his body quakes
in a jelly-like way with interior chuckles; and
at the end of the ten minutes the audience
have laughed until they are exhausted, and
the tears are running down their faces.

The simplicity and innocence and sincerity
and unconsciousness of the old farmer are perfectly simulated, and the result is a performance which is thoroughly charming and delicious. This is art—and fine and beautiful,
and only a master can compass it; but a machine could tell the other story.

To string incongruities and absurdities together in a wandering and sometimes purpose-
less way, and seem innocently unaware that
they are absurdities, is the basis of the American art, if my position is correct. Another
feature is the slurring of the point. A third
is the dropping of a studied remark apparently without knowing it, as if one were thinking
aloud. The fourth and last is the pause.

Artemus Ward dealt in numbers three and
four a good deal. He would begin to tell
with great animation something which he
seemed to think was wonderful; then lose
confidence, and after an apparently absent-
minded pause add an incongruous remark in

a soliloquizing way; and that was the remark
intended to explode the mine—and it did.

For instance, he would say eagerly, excited-
ly, "I once knew a man in New Zealand who
hadn't a tooth in his head"—here his animation would die out; a silent, reflective pause
would follow, then he would say dreamily, and
as if to himself, "and yet that man could beat
a drum better than any man I ever saw."

The pause is an exceedingly important feature in any kind of story, and a frequently re-
curring feature, too. It is a dainty thing, and
delicate, and also uncertain and treacherous;
for it must be exactly the right length — no
more and no less—or it fails of its purpose and
makes trouble. If the pause is too short the
impressive point is passed, and the audience
have had time to divine that a surprise is intended—and then you can't surprise them, of
course.

On the platform I used to tell a negro ghost
story that had a pause in front of the snapper
on the end, and that pause was the most important thing in the whole story. If I got it
the right length precisely, I could spring the
finishing ejaculation with effect enough to
make some impressible girl deliver a startled
little yelp and jump out of her seat—and that

was what I was after. This story was called
" The Golden Arm," and was told in this fashion. You can practise with it yourself—and
mind you look out for the pause and get it
right.

THE GOLDEN ARM

Once 'pon a time dey wuz a monsus mean
man, en he live 'way out in de prairie all 'lone
by hisself, 'cep'n he had a wife. En bimeby
she died, en he tuck en toted her way out dah
in de prairie en buried her. Well, she had a
golden arm—all solid gold, fum de shoulder
down. He wuz pow'ful mean — pow'ful; en
dat night he couldn't sleep, caze he want dat
golden arm so bad.

When it come midnight he couldn't stan' it
no mo'; so he git up, he did, en tuck his lan-
tern en shoved out thoo de storm en dug her
up en got de golden arm; en he bent his head
down 'gin de win', en plowed en plowed en
plowed thoo de snow. Den all on a sudden
he stop (make a considerable pause here, and
look startled, and take a listening attitude) en
say : " My *lan*', what's dat !"

En he listen—en listen—en de win' say (set
your teeth together and imitate the wailing
and wheezing singsong of the wind), " Bzzz-z-

zzz "—en den, way back yonder whah de grave
is, he hear a *voice !*—he hear a voice all mix'
up in de win'— can't hardly tell 'em 'part —
" Bzzz-zzz — W-h-o — g-o-t — m-y — g-o-l-d-e-n
arm ?—zzz—zzz—W-h-o g-o-t m-y g-o-l-d-e-n
arm ? (You must begin to shiver violently
now.)

En he begin to shiver en shake, en say, " Oh,
my! *Oh*, my lan'!" en de win' blow de lan-
tern out, en de snow en sleet blow in his face
en mos' choke him, en he start a-plowin' knee-
deep towards home mos' dead, he so sk'yerd
— en pooty soon he hear de voice agin, en
(pause) it 'us comin' *after* him! " Bzzz—zzz—
zzz—W-h-o—g-o-t—m-y—g-o-l-d-e-n—*arm ?*"

When he git to de pasture he hear it agin—
closter now, en a-*comin'!*—a-comin' back dah
in de dark en de storm—(repeat the wind and
the voice). When he git to de house he rush
up-stairs en jump in de bed en kiver up, head
and years, en lay dah shiverin' en shakin'—en
den way out dah he hear it *agin!*— en a-
comin'! En bimeby he hear (pause — awed,
listening attitude)— pat — pat — pat —*hit's a-
comin' up-stairs !* Den he hear de latch, en he
know it's in de room !

Den pooty soon he know it's a-*stannin' by
de bed!* (Pause.) Den—he know it's a-*bendin'*

down over him—en he cain't skasely git his breath! Den—den—he seem to feel someth'n *c-o-l-d*, right down 'most agin his head! (Pause.)

Den de voice say, *right at his year*—" W-h-o —g-o-t—m-y—g-o-l-d-e-n *arm ?*" (You must wail it out very plaintively and accusingly; then you stare steadily and impressively into the face of the farthest-gone auditor—a girl, preferably—and let that awe-inspiring pause begin to build itself in the deep hush. When it has reached exactly the right length, jump suddenly at that girl and yell, " *You've* got it !"

If you've got the *pause* right, she'll fetch a dear little yelp and spring right out of her shoes. But you *must* get the pause right; and you will find it the most troublesome and aggravating and uncertain thing you ever undertook.)

IN DEFENCE OF HARRIET SHELLEY

IN DEFENCE OF HARRIET SHELLEY

I

I HAVE committed sins, of course; but I have not committed enough of them to entitle me to the punishment of reduction to the bread and water of ordinary literature during six years when I might have been living on the fat diet spread for the righteous in Professor Dowden's *Life of Shelley*, if I had been justly dealt with.

During these six years I have been living a life of peaceful ignorance. I was not aware that Shelley's first wife was unfaithful to him, and that that was why he deserted her and wiped the stain from his sensitive honor by entering into soiled relations with Godwin's young daughter. This was all new to me when I heard it lately, and was told that the proofs of it were in this book, and that this book's verdict is accepted in the girls' colleges of America and its view taught in their literary classes.

In each of these six years multitudes of young people in our country have arrived at the Shelley-reading age. Are these six multitudes unacquainted with this life of Shelley? Perhaps they are; indeed, one may feel pretty sure that the great bulk of them are. To these, then, I address myself, in the hope that some account of this romantic historical fable and the fabulist's manner of constructing and adorning it may interest them.

First, as to its literary style. Our negroes in America have several ways of entertaining themselves which are not found among the whites anywhere. Among these inventions of theirs is one which is particularly popular with them. It is a competition in elegant deportment. They hire a hall and bank the spectators' seats in rising tiers along the two sides, leaving all the middle stretch of the floor free. A cake is provided as a prize for the winner in the competition, and a bench of experts in deportment is appointed to award it. Sometimes there are as many as fifty contestants, male and female, and five hundred spectators. One at a time the contestants enter, clothed regardless of expense in what each considers the perfection of style and taste, and walk down the vacant central space and back again with that multitude of critical eyes on them. All that the competitor knows of fine airs and graces he throws into his carriage, all that he knows of seductive expression he throws into his countenance. He may use all the helps he can devise: watch-chain to twirl with his fingers, cane to do graceful things with, snowy handkerchief to flourish and get artful effects out of, shiny new stovepipe hat to assist in his courtly bows; and the colored lady may have a fan to work up *her* effects with, and smile over and blush behind, and she may add other helps, according to her judgment. When the review by individual detail is over, a grand review of all the contestants in procession follows, with all the airs and graces and all the bowings and smirkings on exhibition at once, and this enables the bench of experts to make the necessary comparisons and arrive at a verdict. The successful competitor gets the prize which I have before mentioned, and an abundance of applause and envy along with it. The negroes have a name for this grave deportment-tournament; a name taken from the prize contended for. They call it a Cake-Walk.

This Shelley biography is a literary cakewalk. The ordinary forms of speech are ab-

2

sent from it.   All the pages, all the para-
graphs, walk by sedately, elegantly, not to say
mincingly, in their Sunday-best, shiny and
sleek, perfumed, and with *boutonnières* in their
button-holes; it is rare to find even a chance
sentence that has forgotten to dress.   If the
book wishes to tell us that Mary Godwin,
child of sixteen, had known afflictions, the fact
saunters forth in this nobby outfit: "Mary
was herself not unlearned in the lore of pain"
—meaning by that that she had not always
travelled on asphalt; or, as some authorities
would frame it, that she had "been there herself," a form which, while preferable to the
book's form, is still not to be recommended.
If the book wishes to tell us that Harriet
Shelley hired a wet-nurse, that commonplace
fact gets turned into a dancing-master, who
does his professional bow before us in pumps
and knee-breeches, with his fiddle under one
arm and his crush-hat under the other, thus:
"The beauty of Harriet's motherly relation to
her babe was marred in Shelley's eyes by the
introduction into his house of a hireling nurse
to whom was delegated the mother's tenderest
office."

This is perhaps the strangest book that has
seen the light since Frankenstein.   Indeed, it

is a Frankenstein itself; a Frankenstein with
the original infirmity supplemented by a new
one; a Frankenstein with the reasoning faculty wanting. Yet it believes it can reason, and
is always trying. It is not content to leave a
mountain of fact standing in the clear sun-
shine, where the simplest reader can perceive
its form, its details, and its relation to the rest
of the landscape, but thinks it must help him
examine it and understand it; so its drifting
mind settles upon it with that intent, but always with one and the same result: there is a
change of temperature and the mountain is
hid in a fog. Every time it sets up a premise
and starts to reason from it, there is a surprise
in store for the reader. It is strangely near-
sighted, cross-eyed, and purblind. Sometimes
when a mastodon walks across the field of its
vision it takes it for a rat; at other times it
does not see it at all.

The materials of this biographical fable are
facts, rumors, and poetry. They are connected together and harmonized by the help of
suggestion, conjecture, innuendo, perversion,
and semi-suppression.

The fable has a distinct object in view, but
this object is not acknowledged in set words.
Percy Bysshe Shelley has done something

which in the case of other men is called a grave crime; it must be shown that in his case it is not that, because he does not think as other men do about these things.

Ought not that to be enough, if the fabulist is serious? Having proved that a crime is not a crime, was it worth while to go on and fasten the responsibility of a crime which was not a crime upon somebody else? What is the use of hunting down and holding to bitter account people who are responsible for other people's innocent acts?

Still, the fabulist thinks it a good idea to do that. In his view Shelley's first wife, Harriet, free of all offence as far as we have historical facts for guidance, must be held unforgivably responsible for her husband's innocent act in deserting her and taking up with another woman.

Any one will suspect that this task has its difficulties. Any one will divine that nice work is necessary here, cautious work, wily work, and that there is entertainment to be had in watching the magician do it. There is indeed entertainment in watching him. He arranges his facts, his rumors, and his poems on his table in full view of the house, and shows you that everything is there—no decep-

tion, everything fair and aboveboard. And
this is apparently true, yet there is a defect,
for some of his best stock is hid in an appendix-basket behind the door, and you do not
come upon it until the exhibition is over and
the enchantment of your mind accomplished
—as the magician thinks.

There is an insistent atmosphere of candor
and fairness about this book which is engaging at first, then a little burdensome, then a
trifle fatiguing, then progressively suspicious,
annoying, irritating, and oppressive. It takes
one some little time to find out that phrases
which seem intended to guide the reader
aright are there to mislead him; that phrases
which seem intended to throw light are there
to throw darkness; that phrases which seem
intended to interpret a fact are there to mis-
interpret it; that phrases which seem intended to forestall prejudice are there to create it;
that phrases which seem antidotes are poisons
in disguise. The naked facts arrayed in the
book establish Shelley's guilt in that one episode which disfigures his otherwise superla-
tively lofty and beautiful life; but the historian's careful and methodical misinterpretation
of them transfers the responsibility to the
wife's shoulders—as he persuades himself.

The few meagre facts of Harriet Shelley's life, as furnished by the book, acquit her of offence; but by calling in the forbidden helps of rumor, gossip, conjecture, insinuation, and innuendo he destroys her character and rehabilitates Shelley's—as he believes. And in truth his unheroic work has not been barren of the results he aimed at; as witness the assertion made to me that girls in the colleges of America are taught that Harriet Shelley put a stain upon her husband's honor, and that that was what stung him into repurifying himself by deserting her and his child and entering into scandalous relations with a school-girl acquaintance of his.

If that assertion is true, they probably use a reduction of this work in those colleges, maybe only a sketch outlined from it. Such a thing as that could be harmful and misleading. They ought to cast it out and put the whole book in its place. It would not deceive. It would not deceive the janitor.

All of this book is interesting on account of the sorcerer's methods and the attractiveness of some of his characters and the repulsiveness of the rest, but no part of it is so much so as are the chapters wherein he tries to think he thinks he sets forth the causes which led to Shelley's desertion of his wife in 1814.

Harriet Westbrook was a school-girl sixteen years old. Shelley was teeming with advanced thought. He believed that Christianity was a degrading and selfish superstition, and he had a deep and sincere desire to rescue one of his sisters from it. Harriet was impressed by his various philosophies and looked upon him as an intellectual wonder—which indeed he was. He had an idea that she could give him valuable help in his scheme regarding his sister; therefore he asked her to correspond with him. She was quite willing. Shelley was not thinking of love, for he was just getting over a passion for his cousin, Harriet Grove, and just getting well steeped in one for Miss Hitchener, a school-teacher. What might happen to Harriet Westbrook before the letter-writing was ended did not enter his mind. Yet an older person could have made a good guess at it, for in person Shelley was as beautiful as an angel, he was frank, sweet, winning, unassuming, and so rich in unselfishnesses, generosities, and magnanimities that he made his whole generation seem poor in these great qualities by comparison. Besides, he was in distress. His college had expelled him for writing an atheistical pamphlet and afflicting the reverend heads of the university with it, his rich father and grandfather had closed their purses against him, his friends were cold. Necessarily, Harriet fell in love with him ; and so deeply, indeed, that there was no way for Shelley to save her from suicide but to marry her. He believed himself to blame for this state of things, so the marriage took place. He was pretty fairly in love with Harriet, although he loved Miss Hitchener better. He wrote and explained the case to Miss Hitchener after the wedding, and he could not have been franker or more *naïve* and less stirred up about the circumstance if the matter in issue had been a commercial transaction involving thirty-five dollars.

Shelley was nineteen. He was not a youth, but a man. He had never had any youth. He was an erratic and fantastic child during eighteen years, then he stepped into manhood, as one steps over a door-sill. He was curiously mature at nineteen in his ability to do independent thinking on the deep questions of life and to arrive at sharply definite decisions regarding them, and stick to them — stick to them and stand by them at cost of bread, friendships, esteem, respect and approbation.

For the sake of his opinions he was willing
to sacrifice all these valuable things, and did
sacrifice them ; and went on doing it, too,
when he could at any moment have made
himself rich and supplied himself with friends
and esteem by compromising with his father,
at the moderate expense of throwing over-
board one or two indifferent details of his
cargo of principles.

He and Harriet eloped to Scotland and got
married. They took lodgings in Edinburgh
of a sort answerable to their purse, which was
about empty, and there their life was a happy
one and grew daily more so. They had only
themselves for company, but they needed no
additions to it. They were as cozy and contented as birds in a nest. Harriet sang evenings or read aloud ; also she studied and tried
to improve her mind, her husband instructing
her in Latin. She was very beautiful, she was
modest, quiet, genuine, and, according to her
husband's testimony, she had no fine lady airs
or aspirations about her. In Matthew Arnold's
judgment, she was " a pleasing figure."

The pair remained five weeks in Edinburgh,
and then took lodgings in York, where Shelley's college mate, Hogg, lived. Shelley presently ran down to London, and Hogg took

this opportunity to make love to the young wife. She repulsed him, and reported the fact to her husband when he got back. It seems a pity that Shelley did not copy this creditable conduct of hers some time or other when under temptation, so that we might have seen the author of his biography hang the miracle in the skies and squirt rainbows at it.

At the end of the first year of marriage— the most trying year for any young couple, for then the mutual failings are coming one by one to light, and the necessary adjustments are being made in pain and tribulation—Shelley was able to recognize that his marriage venture had been a safe one. As we have seen, his love for his wife had begun in a rather shallow way and with not much force, but now it was become deep and strong, which entitles his wife to a broad credit mark, one may admit. He addresses a long and loving poem to her, in which both passion and worship appear:

Exhibit A

"O thou
Whose dear love gleamed upon the gloomy path
Which this lone spirit travelled,

.   .   .   .

. . . wilt thou not turn

Those spirit-beaming eyes and look on me,
Until I be assured that Earth is Heaven
And Heaven is Earth?

.   .   .   .

Harriet! let death all mortal ties dissolve,
But ours shall not be mortal."

Shelley also wrote a sonnet to her in August of this same year in celebration of her birthday:

Exhibit B

"Ever as now with Love and Virtue's glow
  May thy unwithering soul not cease to burn,
  Still may thine heart with those pure thoughts o'erflow
  Which force from mine such quick and warm return."

Was the girl of seventeen glad and proud and happy? We may conjecture that she was.

That was the year 1812. Another year passed — still happily, still successfully — a child was born in June, 1813, and in September, three months later, Shelley addresses a poem to this child, Ianthe, in which he points out just when the little creature is most particularly dear to him:

Exhibit C

"Dearest when most thy tender traits express
  The image of thy mother's loveliness."

Up to this point the fabulist counsel for Shelley and prosecutor of his young wife has had easy sailing, but now his trouble begins, for Shelley is getting ready to make some unpleasant history for himself, and it will be necessary to put the blame of it on the wife.

Shelley had made the acquaintance of a charming gray-haired, young-hearted Mrs. Boinville, whose face "retained a certain youthful beauty"; she lived at Bracknell, and had a young daughter named Cornelia Turner, who was equipped with many fascinations. Apparently these people were sufficiently sentimental. Hogg says of Mrs. Boinville:

> "The greater part of her associates were odious. I generally found there two or three sentimental young butchers, an eminently philosophical tinker, and several very unsophisticated medical practitioners or medical students, all of low origin and vulgar and offensive manners. They sighed, turned up their eyes, retailed philosophy, such as it was," etc.

Shelley moved to Bracknell, July 27 (this is still 1813), purposely to be near this unwholesome prairie-dogs' nest. The fabulist says: "It was the entrance into a world more amiable and exquisite than he had yet known."

"In this acquaintance the attraction was mutual"—and presently it grew to be very

mutual indeed, between Shelley and Cornelia
Turner, when they got to studying the Italian
poets together.   Shelley, "responding like a
tremulous instrument to every breath of passion or of sentiment," had his chance here.   It
took only four days for Cornelia's attractions
to begin to dim Harriet's.   Shelley arrived on
the 27th of July ; on the 31st he wrote a sonnet to Harriet in which "one detects already
the little rift in the lover's lute which had
seemed to be healed or never to have gaped at
all when the later and happier sonnet to Ianthe
was written"—in September, we remember :

Exhibit D

"EVENING. TO HARRIET

"O thou bright Sun! Beneath the dark blue line
Of western distance that sublime descendest,
And, gleaming lovelier as thy beams decline,
Thy million hues to every vapor lendest,
And over cobweb, lawn, and grove, and stream
Sheddest the liquid magic of thy light,
Till calm Earth, with the parting splendor bright,
Shows like the vision of a beauteous dream ;
What gazer now with astronomic eye
Could coldly count the spots within thy sphere?
Such were thy lover, Harriet, could he fly
The thoughts of all that makes his passion dear,
And turning senseless from thy warm caress
Pick flaws in our close-woven happiness."

I cannot find the "rift"; still it may be there. What the poem *seems* to say, is, that a person would be coldly ungrateful who could consent to count and consider little spots and flaws in such a warm, great, satisfying sun as Harriet is. It is a "little rift which had seemed to be healed, *or* never to have gaped at all." That is, "one *detects*" a little rift which perhaps had never existed. How does one do that? How does one see the invisible? It is the fabulist's secret; he knows how to detect what does not exist, he knows how to see what is not seeable; it is his gift, and he works it many a time to poor dead Harriet Shelley's deep damage.

"As yet, however, if there was a speck upon Shelley's happiness it was no more than a speck"—meaning the one which one detects where "it may never have gaped at all"— "nor had Harriet cause for discontent."

Shelley's Latin instructions to his wife had ceased. "From a teacher he had now become a pupil." Mrs. Boinville and her young married daughter Cornelia were teaching him Italian poetry; a fact which warns one to receive with some caution that other statement that Harriet had no "cause for discontent."

Shelley had stopped instructing Harriet in

Latin, as before mentioned. The biographer thinks that the busy life in London some time back, and the intrusion of the baby, account for this. These were hindrances, but were there no others? He is always overlooking a detail here and there that might be valuable in helping us understand a situation. For instance, when a man has been hard at work at the Italian poets with a pretty woman, hour after hour, and responding like a tremulous instrument to every breath of passion or of sentiment in the meantime, that man is dog-tired when he gets home, and he *can't* teach his wife Latin; it would be unreasonable to expect it.

Up to this time we have submitted to having Mrs. Boinville pushed upon us as ostensibly concerned in these Italian lessons, but the biographer drops her now, of his own accord. Cornelia "perhaps" is sole teacher. Hogg says she was a prey to a kind of sweet melancholy, arising from causes purely imaginary; she required consolation, and found it in Petrarch. He also says, "Bysshe entered at once fully into her views and caught the soft infection, breathing the tenderest and sweetest melancholy, as every true poet ought."

Then the author of the book interlards a

most stately and fine compliment to Cornelia,
furnished by a man of approved judgment who
knew her well "in later years." It is a very
good compliment indeed, and she no doubt
deserved it in her "later years," when she had
for generations ceased to be sentimental and
lackadaisical, and was no longer engaged in
enchanting young husbands and sowing sor-
row for young wives. But why is that compliment to that old gentlewoman intruded
there? Is it to make the reader believe she
was well-chosen and safe society for a young,
sentimental husband? The biographer's device was not well planned. That old person
was not present—it was her other self that was
there, her young, sentimental, melancholy,
warm-blooded self, in those early sweet times
before antiquity had cooled her off and mossed
her back.

"In choosing for friends such women as
Mrs. Newton, Mrs. Boinville, and Cornelia
Turner, Shelley gave good proof of his insight
and discrimination." That is the fabulist's
opinion—Harriet Shelley's is not reported.

Early in August, Shelley was in London trying to raise money. In September he wrote
the poem to the baby, already quoted from.
In the first week of October Shelley and fam-

ily went to Warwick, then to Edinburgh, arriving there about the middle of the month.

"Harriet was happy." Why? The author furnishes a reason, but hides from us whether it is history or conjecture; it is because "*the babe had borne the journey well.*" It has all the aspect of one of his artful devices—flung in in his favorite casual way—the way he has when he wants to draw one's attention away from an obvious thing and amuse it with some trifle that is less obvious but more useful—in a history like this. The obvious thing is, that Harriet was happy because there was much territory between her husband and Cornelia Turner now; and because the perilous Italian lessons were taking a rest; and because, if there chanced to be any respondings like a tremulous instrument to every breath of passion or of sentiment in stock in these days, she might hope to get a share of them herself; and because, with her husband liberated, now, from the fetid fascinations of that sentimental retreat so pitilessly described by Hogg, who also dubbed it "Shelley's paradise" later, she might hope to persuade him to stay away from it permanently; and because she might also hope that his brain would cool, now, and his heart become healthy, and both brain and

3

heart consider the situation and resolve that it would be a right and manly thing to stand by this girl-wife and her child and see that they were honorably dealt with, and cherished and protected and loved by the man that had promised these things, and so be made happy and kept so.   And because, also—may we conjecture this?—we may hope for the privilege of taking up our cozy Latin lessons again, that used to be so pleasant and brought us so near together—so near, indeed, that often our heads touched, just as heads do over Italian lessons; and our hands met in casual and unintentional, but still most delicious and thrilling little contacts and momentary clasps, just as they inevitably do over Italian lessons. Suppose one should say to any young wife: "I find that your husband is poring over the Italian poets and being instructed in the beautiful Italian language by the lovely Cornelia Robinson"— would that cozy picture fail to rise before her mind? would its possibilities fail to suggest themselves to her? would there be a pang in her heart and a blush on her face? or, on the contrary, would the remark give her pleasure, make her joyous and gay? Why, one needs only to make the experiment—the result will not be uncertain.

However, we learn—by authority of deeply reasoned and searching conjecture—that the baby bore the journey well, and that that was why the young wife was happy. That accounts for two per cent. of the happiness, but it was not right to imply that it accounted for the other ninety-eight also.

Peacock, a scholar, poet, and friend of the Shelleys, was of their party when they went away. He used to laugh at the Boinville menagerie, and "was not a favorite." One of the Boinville group, writing to Hogg, said, "The Shelleys have made an addition to their party in the person of a cold scholar, who, I think, has neither taste nor feeling. This, Shelley will perceive sooner or later, for his warm nature craves sympathy." True, and Shelley will fight his way back there to get it —there will be no way to head him off.

Towards the end of November it was necessary for Shelley to pay a business visit to London, and he conceived the project of leaving Harriet and the baby in Edinburgh with Harriet's sister, Eliza Westbrook, a sensible, practical maiden lady about thirty years old, who had spent a great part of her time with the family since the marriage. She was an estimable woman, and Shelley had had reason to

like her, and did like her; but along about this
time his feeling towards her changed.   Part of
Shelley's plan, as he wrote Hogg, was to spend
his London evenings with the Newtons—members of the Boinville Hysterical Society.   But,
alas, when he arrived early in December, that
pleasant game was partially blocked, for Eliza
and the family arrived *with* him.   We are left
destitute of conjectures at this point by the
biographer, and it is my duty to supply one.
I chance the conjecture that it was Eliza who
interfered with that game.   I think she tried
to do what she could towards modifying the
Boinville connection, in the interest of her
young sister's peace and honor.

If it was she who blocked that game, she
was not strong enough to block the next one.
Before the month and year were out—no date
given, let us call it Christmas—Shelley and
family were nested in a furnished house in
Windsor, "at no great distance from the Boinvilles"—these decoys still residing at Bracknell.

What we need, now, is a misleading conjecture.   We get it with characteristic promptness
and depravity:

"But Prince Athanase found not the aged Zonoras,
the friend of his boyhood, in any wanderings to Windsor.   Dr. Lind had died a year since, and with his

death Windsor must have lost, for Shelley, its chief attraction."

Still, not to mention Shelley's wife, there was Bracknell, at any rate. While Bracknell remains, all solace is not lost. Shelley is represented by this biographer as doing a great many careless things, but to my mind this hiring a furnished house for three months in order to be with a man who has been dead a year, is the carelessest of them all. One feels for him—that is but natural, and does us honor besides—yet one is vexed, for all that. He could have written and asked about the aged Zonoras before taking the house. He may not have had the address, but that is nothing —any postman would know the aged Zonoras; a dead postman would remember a name like that.

And yet, why throw a rag like this to us ravening wolves? Is it seriously supposable that we will stop to chew it and let our prey escape? No, we are getting to expect this kind of device, and to give it merely a sniff for certainty's sake and then walk around it and leave it lying. Shelley was not after the aged Zonoras; he was pointed for Cornelia and the Italian lessons, for his warm nature was craving sympathy.

II

THE year 1813 is just ended now, and we step into 1814.

To recapitulate: how much of Cornelia's society has Shelley had, thus far? Portions of August and September, and four days of July. That is to say, he has had opportunity to enjoy it, more or less, during that brief period. Did he want some more of it? We must fall back upon history, and then go to conjecturing.

"In the early part of the year 1814, Shelley was a frequent visitor at Bracknell."

"Frequent" is a cautious word, in this author's mouth; the very cautiousness of it, the vagueness of it, provokes suspicion; it makes one suspect that this frequency was more frequent than the mere common every-day kinds of frequency which one is in the habit of averaging up with the unassuming term "frequent." I think so because they fixed up a bedroom for him in the Boinville house. One doesn't need a bedroom if one is only going to run over now and then in a disconnected way to respond like a tremulous instrument to every breath of passion or of sentiment and rub up one's Italian poetry a little.

The young wife was not invited, perhaps. If she was, she most certainly did not come, or she would have straightened the room up; the most ignorant of us knows that a wife would not endure a room in the condition in which Hogg found this one when he occupied it one night. Shelley was away—why, nobody can divine. Clothes were scattered about, there were books on every side: "Wherever a book could be laid was an open book turned down on its face to keep its place." It seems plain that the wife was not invited. No, not that; I think she was invited, but said to herself that she could not bear to go there and see another young woman touching heads with her husband over an Italian book and making thrilling hand-contacts with him accidentally.

As remarked, he was a frequent visitor there, "where he found an easeful resting-place in the house of Mrs. Boinville—the white-haired Maimuna—and of her daughter, Mrs. Turner." The aged Zonoras was deceased, but the white-haired Maimuna was still on deck, as we see.

"Three charming ladies entertained the mocker (Hogg) with cups of tea, late hours, Wieland's Agathon, sighs and smiles, and the celestial manna of refined sentiment." "Such," says Hogg, "were the delights of Shelley's paradise in Bracknell."

The white-haired Maimuna presently writes to Hogg:

"I will not have you despise home-spun pleasures. Shelley is making a trial of them with us—"

A trial of them. It may be called that. It was March 11, and he had been in the house a month. She continues:

Shelley "likes them so well that he is resolved to leave off rambling—"

But he has *already* left it off. He has been there a month.

"And begin a course of them himself."

But he has already begun it. He has been at it a *month*. He likes it so well that he has forgotten all about his wife, as a letter of his reveals.

"Seriously, I think his mind and body want rest."

Yet he has been resting both for a month, with Italian, and tea, and manna of sentiment, and late hours, and every restful thing a young husband could need for the refreshment of weary limbs and a sore conscience, and a nagging sense of shabbiness and treachery.

"His journeys after what he has never found have racked his purse and his tranquillity. He is resolved to take a little care of the former, in pity to the latter, which I applaud, and shall second with all my might."

But she does not say whether the young wife, a stranger and lonely yonder, wants another woman and her daughter Cornelia to be lavishing so much inflamed interest on her husband or not. That young wife is always silent—we are never allowed to hear from her. She must have opinions about such things, she cannot be indifferent, she must be approving or disapproving, surely she would speak if she were allowed—even to-day and from her grave she would, if she could, I think—but we get only the other side, they keep her silent always.

"He has deeply interested us. In the course of your intimacy he must have made you feel what we now feel for him. He is seeking a house close to us—"

Ah! he is not close enough yet, it seems—

"and if he succeeds we shall have an additional motive to induce you to come among us in the summer."

The reader would puzzle a long time and not guess the biographer's comment upon the above letter. It is this:

"These sound like words of a considerate and judicious friend."

That is what he thinks. That is, it is what he thinks he thinks. No, that is not quite it: it is what he thinks he can stupefy a particularly and unspeakably dull reader into thinking it is what he thinks. He makes that comment with the knowledge that Shelley is in love with this woman's daughter, and that it is because of the fascinations of these two that Shelley has deserted his wife—for this month, considering all the circumstances, and his new passion, and his employment of the time, amounted to desertion; that is its rightful name. We cannot know how the wife regarded it and felt about it; but if she could have read the letter which Shelley was writing to Hogg four or five days later, we could guess her thought and how she felt. Hear him:

.   .   .   .

"I have been staying with Mrs. Boinville for the last month; I have escaped, in the society of all that. philosophy and friendship combine, from the dismaying solitude of myself."

It is fair to conjecture that he was feeling ashamed.

"They have revived in my heart the expiring flame of life. I have felt myself translated to a paradise which has nothing of mortality but its transitoriness; my heart sickens at the view of that necessity which will quickly divide me from the delightful tranquillity of this happy home—for it has become my home.

.   .   .   .

"Eliza is still with us—not here!—but will be with me when the infinite malice of destiny forces me to depart."

Eliza is she who blocked that game—the game in London—the one where we were purposing to dine every night with one of the "three charming ladies" who fed tea and manna and late hours to Hogg at Bracknell.

Shelley could send Eliza away, of course; could have cleared her out long ago if so minded, just as he had previously done with a predecessor of hers whom he had first worshipped and then turned against; but perhaps she was useful there as a thin excuse for staying away himself.

"I am now but little inclined to contest this point. I certainly hate her with all my heart and soul. . . .

"It is a sight which awakens an inexpressible sensation of disgust and horror, to see her caress my poor

little Ianthe, in whom I may hereafter find the consolation of sympathy. I sometimes feel faint with the
fatigue of checking the overflowings of my unbounded
abhorrence for this miserable wretch. But she is no
more than a blind and loathsome worm, that cannot
see to sting.

" I have begun to learn Italian again. . . . Cornelia
assists me in this language. Did I not once tell you
that I thought her cold and reserved? She is the reverse of this, as she is the reverse of everything bad.
She inherits all the divinity of her mother. . . . I
have sometimes forgotten that I am not an inmate of
this delightful home—that a time will come which
will cast me again into the boundless ocean of abhorred society.

" I have written nothing but one stanza, which has
no meaning, and that I have only written in thought:

" Thy dewy looks sink in my breast;
    Thy gentle words stir poison there;
Thou hast disturbed the only rest
    That was the portion of despair.
Subdued to duty's hard control,
    I could have borne my wayward lot:
The chains that bind this ruined soul
    Had cankered then, but crushed it not.

" This is the vision of a delirious and distempered
dream, which passes away at the cold clear light of
morning. Its surpassing excellence and exquisite
perfections have no more reality than the color of an
autumnal sunset."

Then it did not refer to his wife. That is

plain; otherwise he would have said so.   It is well that he explained that it has no meaning, for if he had not done that, the previous soft references to Cornelia and the way he has come to feel about her now would make us think she was the person who had inspired it while teaching him how to read the warm and ruddy Italian poets during a month.

The biography observes that portions of this letter "read like the tired moaning of a wounded creature."   Guesses at the nature of the wound are permissible; we will hazard one.

Read by the light of Shelley's previous history, his letter seems to be the cry of a tortured conscience.   Until this time it was a conscience that had never felt a pang or known a smirch.   It was the conscience of one who, until this time, had never done a dishonorable thing, or an ungenerous, or cruel, or treacherous thing, but was now doing all of these, and was keenly aware of it.   Up to this time Shelley had been master of his nature, and it was a nature which was as beautiful and as nearly perfect as any merely human nature may be. But he was drunk, now, with a debasing passion, and was not himself.   There is nothing in his previous history that is in character with

the Shelley of this letter. He had done boy-
ish things, foolish things, even crazy things,
but never a thing to be ashamed of. He had
done things which one might laugh at, but the
privilege of laughing was limited always to
the thing itself; you could not laugh at the
motive back of it—that was high, that was
noble. His most fantastic and quixotic acts
had a purpose back of them which made them
fine, often great, and made the rising laugh
seem profanation and quenched it; quenched
it, and changed the impulse to homage. Up
to this time he had been loyalty itself, where
his obligations lay—treachery was new to him;
he had never done an ignoble thing—baseness
was new to him; he had never done an unkind thing—that also was new to him.

This was the author of that letter, this was
the man who had deserted his young wife and
was lamenting, because he must leave another
woman's house which had become a "home"
to him, and go away. Is he lamenting *mainly*
because he must go back to his wife and child?
No, the lament is mainly for what he is to
leave behind him. The physical comforts of
the house? No, in his life he had never at-
tached importance to such things. Then the
thing which he grieves to leave is narrowed

down to a person—to the person whose " dewy looks " had sunk into his breast, and whose seducing words had " stirred poison there."

He was ashamed of himself, his conscience was upbraiding him. He was the slave of a degrading love ; he was drunk with his passion, the real Shelley was in temporary eclipse. This is the verdict which his previous history must certainly deliver upon this episode, I think.

One must be allowed to assist himself with conjectures like these when trying to find his way through a literary swamp which has so many misleading finger-boards up as this book is furnished with.

We have now arrived at a part of the swamp where the difficulties and perplexities are going to be greater than any we have yet met with—where, indeed, the finger-boards are multitudinous, and the most of them pointing diligently in the wrong direction. We are to be told by the biography why Shelley deserted his wife and child and took up with Cornelia Turner and Italian. It was not on account of Cornelia's sighs and sentimentalities and tea and manna and late hours and soft and sweet and industrious enticements ; no, it was because " his happiness in his home had been wounded and bruised almost to death."

It had been wounded and bruised almost to death in this way :

1st. Harriet persuaded him to set up a carriage.

2d. After the intrusion of the baby, Harriet stopped reading aloud and studying.

3d. Harriet's walks with Hogg "commonly conducted us to some fashionable bonnet-shop."

4th. Harriet hired a wet-nurse.

5th. When an operation was being performed upon the baby, "Harriet stood by, narrowly observing all that was done, but, to the astonishment of the operator, betraying not the smallest sign of emotion."

6th. Eliza Westbrook, sister-in-law, was still of the household.

The evidence against Harriet Shelley is all in ; there is no more. Upon these six counts she stands indicted of the crime of driving her husband into that sty at Bracknell; and this crime, by these helps, the biographical prosecuting attorney has set himself the task of proving upon her.

Does the biographer *call* himself the attorney for the prosecution ? No, only to himself, privately; publicly he is the passionless, disinterested, impartial judge on the bench.

He holds up his judicial scales before the
world, that all may see; and it all tries to
look so fair that a blind person would sometimes fail to see him slip the false weights in.

Shelley's happiness in his home had been
wounded and bruised almost to death, first,
because Harriet had persuaded him to set up
a carriage. I cannot discover that any evidence is offered that she asked him to set up
a carriage. Still, if she did, was it a heavy
offence? Was it unique? Other young wives
had committed it before, others have committed it since. Shelley had dearly loved her
in those London days; possibly he set up the
carriage gladly to please her; affectionate
young husbands do such things. When Shelley ran away with another girl, by-and-by,
this girl persuaded him to pour the price of
many carriages and many horses down the
bottomless well of her father's debts, but this
impartial judge finds no fault with that. Once
she appeals to Shelley to raise money—necessarily by borrowing, there was no other way—
to pay her father's debts with at a time when
Shelley was in danger of being arrested and
imprisoned for his own debts; yet the good
judge finds no fault with her even for this.

First and last, Shelley emptied into that

4

rapacious mendicant's lap a sum which cost him—for he borrowed it at ruinous rates— from eighty to one hundred thousand dollars. But it was Mary Godwin's papa, the supplications were often sent through Mary, the good judge is Mary's strenuous friend, so Mary gets no censures. On the Continent *Mary rode in her private carriage*, built, as Shelley boasts, "by one of the best makers in Bond Street," yet the good judge makes not even a passing comment on this iniquity. Let us throw out Count No. 1 against Harriet Shelley as being far-fetched and frivolous.

Shelley's happiness in his home had been wounded and bruised almost to death, secondly, because Harriet's studies "had dwindled away to nothing, Bysshe had ceased to express any interest in them." At what time was this? It was when Harriet "had fully recovered from the fatigue of her first effort of maternity, . . . and was now in full force, vigor, and effect." Very well, the baby was born two days before the close of June. It took the mother a month to get back her full force, vigor, and effect; this brings us to July 27th and the deadly Cornelia. If a wife of eighteen is studying with her husband and he gets smitten with another woman, isn't he likely to lose interest in his wife's studies for *that* reason, and is not his wife's interest in her studies likely to languish for the *same* reason? Would not the mere sight of those books of hers sharpen the pain that is in her heart? This sudden breaking down of a mutual intellectual interest of two years' standing is coincident with Shelley's re-encounter with Cornelia; and we are allowed to gather from that time forth for nearly two months he did all his studying in that person's society. We feel at liberty to rule out Count No. 2 from the indictment against Harriet.

Shelley's happiness in his home had been wounded and bruised almost to death, thirdly, because Harriet's walks with Hogg commonly led to some fashionable bonnet-shop. I offer no palliation; I only ask why the dispassionate, impartial judge did not offer one himself —merely, I mean, to offset his leniency in a similar case or two where the girl who ran away with Harriet's husband was the shopper. There are several occasions where she interested herself with shopping—among them being walks which ended at the bonnet-shop— yet in none of these cases does she get a word of blame from the good judge, while in one of them he covers the deed with a justifying remark, she doing the shopping that time to

find easement for her mind, her child having
died.

Shelley's happiness in his home had been
wounded and bruised almost to death, fourth-
ly, by the introduction there of a wet-nurse.
The wet-nurse was introduced at the time
of the Edinburgh sojourn, immediately after
Shelley had been enjoying the two months of
study with Cornelia which broke up his wife's
studies and destroyed his personal interest in
them. Why, by this time, nothing that Shelley's wife could do would have been satisfactory to him, for he was in love with another
woman, and was never going to be contented
again until he got back to her. If he had
been still in love with his wife it is not easily
conceivable that he would care much who
nursed the baby, provided the baby was well
nursed. Harriet's jealousy was assuredly voic-
ing itself now, Shelley's conscience was assuredly nagging him, pestering him, persecuting
him. Shelley needed excuses for his altered
attitude towards his wife; Providence pitied
him and sent the wet-nurse. If Providence
had sent him a cotton doughnut it would have
answered just as well; all he wanted was something to find fault with.

Shelley's happiness in his home had been

wounded and bruised almost to death, fifthly,
because Harriet narrowly watched a surgical
operation which was being performed upon
her child, and, "to the astonishment of the
operator," who was watching Harriet instead
of attending to his operation, she betrayed
"not the smallest sign of emotion." The author of this biography was not ashamed to set
down that exultant slander. He was apparently not aware that it was a small business
to bring into his court a witness whose name
he does not know, and whose character and
veracity there is none to vouch for, and allow
him to strike this blow at the mother-heart of
this friendless girl. The biographer says, "We
may not infer from this that Harriet did not
feel "—why put it in, then?—"but we learn
that those about her could believe her to be
hard and insensible." Who were those who
were about her? Her husband? He hated
her now, because he was in love elsewhere.
Her sister? Of course that is not charged.
Peacock? Peacock does not testify. The
wet-nurse? She does not testify. If any
others were there we have no mention of
them. "Those about her" are reduced to one
person—her husband. Who reports the circumstance? It is Hogg. Perhaps he was

there—we do not know.   But if he was, he
still got his information at second-hand, as it
was the operator who noticed Harriet's lack of
emotion, not himself.   Hogg is not given to
saying kind things when Harriet is his subject.
He may have said them the time that he tried
to tempt her to soil her honor, but after that
he mentions her usually with a sneer.   "Among
those who were about her" was one witness
well equipped to silence all tongues, abolish
all doubts, set our minds at rest; one witness,
not called and not callable, whose evidence, if
we could but get it, would outweigh the oaths
of whole battalions of hostile Hoggs and name-
less surgeons—the baby.   I wish we had the
baby's testimony; and yet if we had it it would
not do us any good—a furtive conjecture, a
sly insinuation, a pious "if" or two, would be
smuggled in, here and there, with a solemn air
of judicial investigation, and its positiveness
would wilt into dubiety.

The biographer says of Harriet, "If words
of tender affection and motherly pride prove
the reality of love, then undoubtedly she loved
her first-born child."   That is, if mere empty
words can prove it, it stands proved—and in
this way, without committing himself, he gives
the reader a chance to infer that there isn't

any extant evidence but words, and that he
doesn't take much stock in them. How seldom he shows his hand! He is always lurk-
ing behind a non-committal " if " or something
of that kind; always gliding and dodging
around, distributing colorless poison here and
there and everywhere, but always leaving himself in a position to say that his language will
be found innocuous if taken to pieces and examined. He clearly exhibits a steady and
never-relaxing purpose to make Harriet the
scapegoat for her husband's first great sin—
but it is in the general view that this is revealed, not in the details. His insidious literature is like blue water; you know what it is
that makes it blue, but you cannot produce
and verify any detail of the cloud of micro-
scopic dust in it that does it. Your adversary
can dip up a glassful and show you that it is
pure white and you cannot deny it; and he
can dip the lake dry, glass by glass, and show
that every glassful is white, and prove it to
any one's eye—and yet that lake *was* blue and
you can swear it. This book is blue—with
slander in solution.

Let the reader examine, for example, the
paragraph of comment which immediately follows the letter containing Shelley's self-expos-

ure which we have been considering. This is
it. One should inspect the individual sentences as they go by, then pass them in procession and review the cake-walk as a whole:

> "Shelley's happiness in his home, as is evident from
> this pathetic letter, had been fatally stricken; it is
> evident, also, that he knew where duty lay; he felt
> that his part was to take up his burden, silently and
> sorrowfully, and to bear it henceforth with the quiet-
> ness of despair. But we can perceive that he scarcely
> possessed the strength and fortitude needful for suc-
> cess in such an attempt. And clearly Shelley himself
> was aware how perilous it was to accept that respite
> of blissful ease which he enjoyed in the Boinville
> household; for gentle voices and dewy looks and
> words of sympathy could not fail to remind him of an
> ideal of tranquillity or of joy which could never be
> his, and which he must henceforth sternly exclude
> from his imagination."

That paragraph commits the author in no
way. Taken sentence by sentence it *asserts*
nothing against anybody or in favor of anybody, pleads for nobody, accuses nobody.
Taken detail by detail, it is as innocent as
moonshine. And yet, taken as a whole, it is
a design against the reader; its intent is to
remove the feeling which the letter must leave
with him if let alone, and put a different one
in its place—to remove a feeling justified by

the letter and substitute one not justified by
it. The letter itself gives you no uncertain
picture — no lecturer is needed to stand by
with a stick and point out its details and let
on to explain what they mean. The picture
is the very clear and remorsefully faithful
picture of a fallen and fettered angel who is
ashamed of himself; an angel who beats his
soiled wings and cries, who complains to the
woman who enticed him that he *could* have
borne his wayward lot, he *could* have stood by
his duty if it had not been for her beguile-
ments; an angel who rails at the " boundless
ocean of abhorred society," and rages at his
poor judicious sister - in - law. If there is any
dignity about this spectacle it will escape most
people.

Yet when the paragraph of comment is
taken as a whole, the picture is full of dignity
and pathos; we have before us a blameless
and noble spirit stricken to the earth by ma-
lign powers, but not conquered; tempted, but
grandly putting the temptation away; en-
meshed by subtle coils, but sternly resolved to
rend them and march forth victorious, at any
peril of life or limb. Curtain—slow music.

Was it the purpose of the paragraph to take
the bad taste of Shelley's letter out of the read-

er's mouth? If that was not it, good ink was wasted; without that, it has no relevancy— the multiplication table would have padded the space as rationally.

We have inspected the six reasons which we are asked to believe drove a man of conspicuous patience, honor, justice, fairness, kindliness, and iron firmness, resolution, and steadfastness, from the wife whom he loved and who loved him, to a refuge in the mephitic paradise of Bracknell. These are six infinitely little reasons; but there were six colossal ones, and these the counsel for the destruction of Harriet Shelley persists in not considering very important.

Moreover, the colossal six preceded the little six, and had done the mischief before they were born. Let us double-column the twelve; then we shall see at a glance that each little reason is in turn answered by a retorting reason of a size to overshadow it and make it insignificant:

1. Harriet sets up carriage.	1. CORNELIA TURNER.
2. Harriet stops studying.	2. CORNELIA TURNER.
3. Harriet goes to bonnet-shop.	3. CORNELIA TURNER.
4. Harriet takes a wet-nurse.	4. CORNELIA TURNER.
5. Harriet has too much nerve.	5. CORNELIA TURNER.
6. Detested sister-in-law.	6. CORNELIA TURNER.

As soon as we comprehend that Cornelia
Turner and the Italian lessons happened *before*
the little six had been discovered to be griev-
ances, we understand why Shelley's happiness
in his home had been wounded and bruised
almost to death, and no one can persuade us
into laying it on Harriet. Shelley and Cornelia are the responsible persons, and we cannot in honor and decency allow the cruelties
which they practised upon the unoffending
wife to be pushed aside in order to give us a
chance to waste time and tears over six sentimental justifications of an offence which the
six can't justify, nor even respectably assist
in justifying.

Six? There were seven; but in charity to
the biographer the seventh ought not to be
exposed. Still, he hung it out himself, and
not only hung it out, but thought it was a
good point in Shelley's favor. For two years
Shelley found sympathy and intellectual food
and all that at home; there was enough for
spiritual and mental support, but not enough
for luxury; and so, at the end of the contented two years, this latter detail justifies him
in going bag and baggage over to Cornelia
Turner and supplying the rest of his need in
the way of surplus sympathy and intellectual

pie unlawfully. By the same reasoning a man
in merely comfortable circumstances may rob
a bank without sin.

III

IT is 1814, it is the 16th of March, Shelley
has written his letter, he has been in the Boinville paradise a month, his deserted wife is in
her husbandless home. Mischief had been
wrought. It is the biographer who concedes
this. We greatly need some light on Harriet's
side of the case now; we need to know how
she enjoyed the month, but there is no way
to inform ourselves; there seems to be a
strange absence of documents and letters and
diaries on that side. Shelley kept a diary,
the approaching Mary Godwin kept a diary,
her father kept one, her half-sister by marriage,
adoption, and the dispensation of God kept
one, and the entire tribe and all its friends
wrote and received letters, and the letters were
kept and are producible when this biography
needs them; but there are only three or four
scraps of Harriet's writing, and no diary. Harriet wrote plenty of letters to her husband—
nobody knows where they are, I suppose; she

wrote plenty of letters to other people—apparently they have disappeared, too. Peacock says she wrote good letters, but apparently interested people had sagacity enough to mislay them in time. After all her industry she went down into her grave and lies silent there—silent, when she has so much need to speak. We can only wonder at this mystery, not account for it.

No, there is no way of finding out what Harriet's state of feeling was during the month that Shelley was disporting himself in the Bracknell paradise. We have to fall back upon conjecture, as our fabulist does when he has nothing more substantial to work with. Then we easily conjecture that as the days dragged by Harriet's heart grew heavier and heavier under its two burdens—shame and resentment: the shame of being pointed at and gossiped about as a deserted wife, and resentment against the woman who had beguiled her husband from her and now kept him in a disreputable captivity. Deserted wives — deserted whether for cause or without cause—find small charity among the virtuous and the discreet. We conjecture that one after another the neighbors ceased to call; that one after another they got to being " engaged " when

Harriet called; that finally they one after the other cut her dead on the street; that after that she stayed in the house daytimes, and brooded over her sorrows, and night-times did the same, there being nothing else to do with the heavy hours and the silence and solitude and the dreary intervals which sleep should have charitably bridged, but didn't.

Yes, mischief had been wrought. The biographer arrives at this conclusion, and it is a most just one. Then, just as you begin to half hope he is going to discover the cause of it and launch hot bolts of wrath at the guilty manufacturers of it, you have to turn away disappointed. You are disappointed, and you sigh. This is what he says — the italics are mine:

"However the mischief may have been wrought— *and at this day no one can wish to heap blame on any buried head—*"

So it is poor Harriet, after all. Stern justice must take its course — justice tempered with delicacy, justice tempered with compassion, justice that pities a forlorn dead girl and refuses to strike her. Except in the back. Will not be ignoble and *say* the harsh thing, but only insinuate it. Stern justice knows about the carriage and the wet-nurse and the bonnet-shop and the other dark things that caused this sad mischief, and may not, *must* not blink them; so it delivers judgment where judgment belongs, but softens the blow by not seeming to deliver judgment at all. To resume—the italics are mine:

"However the mischief may have been wrought— and at this day no one can wish to heap blame on any buried head—*it is certain that some cause or causes of deep division between Shelley and his wife were in operation during the early part of the year* 1814."

This shows penetration. No deduction could be more accurate than this. There were indeed some causes of deep division. But next comes another disappointing sentence:

"To guess at the precise nature of these causes, in the absence of definite statement, were useless."

Why, he has already been guessing at them for several pages, and we have been trying to outguess him, and now all of a sudden he is tired of it and won't play any more. It is not quite fair to us. However, he will get over this by-and-by, when Shelley commits his next indiscretion and has to be guessed out of it at Harriet's expense.

"We may rest content with Shelley's own words"—in a Chancery paper drawn up by him three years later. They were these: "Delicacy forbids me to say more than that we were disunited by incurable dissensions."

As for me, I do not quite see why we should rest content with anything of the sort. It is not a very definite statement. It does not necessarily mean anything more than that he did not wish to go into the tedious details of those family quarrels. Delicacy could quite properly excuse him from saying, "I was in love with Cornelia all that time; my wife kept crying and worrying about it and upbraiding me and begging me to cut myself free from a connection which was wronging her and disgracing us both; and I being stung by these reproaches retorted with fierce and bitter speeches—for it is my nature to do that when I am stirred, especially if the target of them is a person whom I had greatly loved and respected before, as witness my various attitudes towards Miss Hitchener, the Gisbornes, Harriet's sister, and others—and finally I did not improve this state of things when I deserted my wife and spent a whole month with the woman who had infatuated me."

No, he could not go into those details, and

we excuse him; but, nevertheless, we do not
rest content with this bland proposition to
puff away that whole long disreputable episode
with a single meaningless remark of Shelley's.

We do admit that "it is certain that some
cause or causes of deep division were in operation." We would admit it just the same if
the grammar of the statement were as straight
as a string, for we drift into pretty indifferent
grammar ourselves when we are absorbed in
historical work; but we have to decline to
admit that we cannot guess those cause or
causes.

But guessing is not really necessary. There
is evidence attainable—evidence from the batch
discredited by the biographer and set out at
the back door in his appendix-basket; and
yet a court of law would think twice before
throwing it out, whereas it would be a hardy
person who would venture to offer in such a
place a good part of the material which is
placed before the readers of this book as "evidence," and so treated by this daring biographer. Among some letters (in the appendix-
basket) from Mrs. Godwin, detailing the God-
winian share in the Shelleyan events of 1814,
she tells how Harriet Shelley came to her and
her husband, agitated and weeping, to implore

5

them to forbid Shelley the house, and prevent
his seeing Mary Godwin.

" She related that last November he had fallen in
love with Mrs. Turner and paid her such marked at-
tentions Mr. Turner, the husband, had carried off his
wife to Devonshire."

The biographer finds a technical fault in
this; " the Shelleys were in *Edinburgh* in November." What of that? The woman is recalling a conversation which is more than two
months old; besides, she was probably more
intent upon the central and important fact of
it than upon its unimportant date. Harriet's
quoted statement has some sense in it; for
that reason, if for no other, it ought to have
been put in the body of the book. Still, that
would not have answered; even the biographer's enemy could not be cruel enough to
ask him to let this real grievance, this compact and substantial and picturesque figure,
this rawhead-and-bloody-bones, come striding
in there among those pale shams, those rickety
spectres labelled WET-NURSE, BONNET-SHOP,
and so on—no, the father of all malice could
not ask the biographer to expose his pathetic
goblins to a competition like that.

The fabulist finds fault with the statement

because it has a technical error in it; and he does this at the moment that he is furnishing us an error himself, and of a graver sort. He says:

"If Turner carried off his wife to Devonshire he brought her back, and Shelley was staying with her and her mother on terms of cordial intimacy in March, 1814."

We accept the "cordial intimacy"—it was the very thing Harriet was complaining of—but there is nothing to show that it was Turner who brought his wife back. The statement is thrown in as if it were not only true, but was proof that Turner was not uneasy. Turner's *movements* are proof of nothing. Nothing but a statement from Turner's mouth would have any value here, and he made none.

Six days after writing his letter Shelley and his wife were together again for a moment— to get remarried according to the rites of the English Church.

Within three weeks the new husband and wife were apart again, and the former was back in his odorous paradise. This time it is the wife who does the deserting. She finds Cornelia too strong for her, probably. At any rate, she goes away with her baby and sister, and we have a playful fling at her from good

Mrs. Boinville, the "mysterious spinner Maimuna"; she whose "face was as a damsel's face, and yet her hair was gray"; she of whom the biographer has said, "Shelley was indeed caught in an almost invisible thread spun around him, but unconsciously, by this subtle and benignant enchantress." The subtle and benignant enchantress writes to Hogg, April 18: "Shelley is again a widower; his beauteous half went to town on Thursday."

Then Shelley writes a poem—a chant of grief over the hard fate which obliges him now to leave his paradise and take up with his wife again. It seems to intimate that the paradise is cooling towards him; that he is warned off by acclamation; that he must not even venture to tempt with one last tear his friend Cornelia's ungentle mood, for her eye is glazed and cold and dares not entreat her lover to stay:

Exhibit E

.   .   .   .

"Pause not! the time is past! Every voice cries
   'Away!'
  Tempt not with one last tear thy friend's ungentle
    mood;
  Thy lover's eye, so glazed and cold, dares not entreat thy stay:
  Duty and dereliction guide thee back to solitude."

Back to the solitude of his now empty home, that is!

> "Away! away! to thy sad and silent home;
> Pour bitter tears on its desolated hearth."

>   .   .   .   .

But he will have rest in the grave by-and-by. Until that time comes, the charms of Bracknell will remain in his memory, along with Mrs. Boinville's voice and Cornelia Turner's smile:

> "Thou in the grave shalt rest — yet, till the phantoms flee
>   Which that house and hearth and garden made dear to thee erewhile,
> Thy remembrance and repentance and deep musings are not free
>   From the music of two voices and the light of one sweet smile."

We *cannot* wonder that Harriet could not stand it. Any of us would have left. We would not even stay with a cat that was in this condition. Even the Boinvilles could not endure it; and so, as we have seen, they gave this one notice.

> "Early in May, Shelley was in London. He did not yet despair of reconciliation with Harriet, nor had he ceased to love her."

Shelley's poems are a good deal of trouble to his biographer. They are constantly inserted as "evidence," and they make much confusion. As soon as one of them has proved one thing, another one follows and proves quite a different thing. The poem just quoted shows that he was in love with Cornelia, but a month later he is in love with Harriet again, and there is a poem to prove it.

"In this piteous appeal Shelley declares that he has now no grief but one—the grief of having known and lost his wife's love."

Exhibit F

"Thy look of love has power to calm
The stormiest passion of my soul."

But without doubt she had been reserving her looks of love a good part of the time for ten months, now—ever since he began to lavish his own on Cornelia Turner at the end of the previous July. He does really seem to have already forgotten Cornelia's merits in one brief month, for he eulogizes Harriet in a way which rules all competition out:

"Thou only virtuous, gentle, kind,
Amid a world of hate."

He complains of her hardness, and begs her

to make the concession of a "slight endur-
ance"—of his waywardness, perhaps—for the
sake of "a fellow-being's lasting weal." But
the main force of his appeal is in his closing
stanza, and is strongly worded :

> "O trust for once no erring guide!
>   Bid the remorseless feeling flee;
> 'Tis malice, 'tis revenge, 'tis pride,
>   'Tis anything but thee;
> O deign a nobler pride to prove,
> And pity if thou canst not love."

This is in May—apparently towards the end
of it. Harriet and Shelley were corresponding all the time. Harriet got the poem — a
copy exists in her own handwriting; she being the only gentle and kind person amid a
world of hate, according to Shelley's own testimony in the poem, we are permitted to think
that the daily letters would presently have
melted that kind and gentle heart and brought
about the reconciliation, if there had been time
—but there wasn't : for in a very few days—
in fact, before the 8th of June—Shelley was in
love with *another* woman !

And so—perhaps while Harriet was walking
the floor nights, trying to get *her* poem by
heart—her husband was doing a fresh one—

for the other girl—Mary Wollstonecraft Godwin—with sentiments like these in it:

Exhibit G

"To spend years thus and be rewarded,
  As thou, sweet love, requited me
  When none were near.
  . . . thy lips did meet
  Mine tremblingly; . . .

"Gentle and good and mild thou art,
  Nor can I live if thou appear
  Aught but thyself.". . .

And so on. "Before the close of June it was
known and felt by Mary and Shelley that each
was inexpressibly dear to the other." Yes,
Shelley had found this child of sixteen to his
liking, and had wooed and won her in the
graveyard. But that is nothing; it was better
than wooing her in her nursery, at any rate,
where it might have disturbed the other children.

However, she was a child in years only.
From the day that she set her masculine grip
on Shelley he was to frisk no more. If she
had occupied the only kind and gentle Harriet's place in March it would have been a
thrilling spectacle to see her invade the Boinville rookery and read the riot act. That holi-

day of Shelley's would have been of short
duration, and Cornelia's hair would have been
as gray as her mother's when the services were
over.

Hogg went to the Godwin residence in
Skinner Street with Shelley on that 8th of
June. They passed through Godwin's little
debt-factory of a book-shop and went up-stairs
hunting for the proprietor. Nobody there.
Shelley strode about the room impatiently,
making its crazy floor quake under him. Then
a door "was partially and softly opened. A
thrilling voice called, 'Shelley!' A thrilling
voice answered, 'Mary!' And he darted out
of the room like an arrow from the bow of the
far-shooting King. A very young female, fair
and fair-haired, pale indeed, and with a piercing look, wearing a frock of tartan, an unusual
dress in London at that time, had called him
out of the room."

This is Mary Godwin, as described by Hogg.
The thrill of the voices shows that the love of
Shelley and Mary was already upward of a
fortnight old; therefore it had been born within the month of May—born while Harriet was
still trying to get her poem by heart, we think.
I must not be asked how I know so much
about that thrill; it is my secret. The biog-

rapher and I have private ways of finding out
things when it is necessary to find them out
and the customary methods fail.

Shelley left London that day, and was gone
ten days. The biographer conjectures that he
spent this interval with Harriet in Bath. It
would be just like him. To the end of his
days he liked to be in love with two women at
once. He was more in love with Miss Hitchener when he married Harriet than he was
with Harriet, and told the lady so with simple
and unostentatious candor. He was more in
love with Cornelia than he was with Harriet
in the end of 1813 and the beginning of 1814,
yet he supplied both of them with love poems
of an equal temperature meantime; he loved
Mary and Harriet in June, and while getting
ready to run off with the one, it is conjectured
that he put in his odd time trying to get reconciled to the other; by-and-by, while still
in love with Mary, he will make love to her
half-sister by marriage, adoption, and the visi-
tation of God, through the medium of clandes-
tine letters, and she will answer with letters
that are for no eye but his own.

When Shelley encountered Mary Godwin
he was looking around for another paradise.
He had tastes of his own, and there were feat-

ures about the Godwin establishment that
strongly recommended it.   Godwin was an advanced thinker and an able writer.   One of
his romances is still read, but his philosophical
works, once so esteemed, are out of vogue
now; their authority was already declining
when Shelley made his acquaintance — that
is, it was declining with the public, but not
with Shelley.   They had been his moral and
political Bible, and they were that yet.   Shelley the infidel would himself have claimed to
be less a work of God than a work of Godwin.
Godwin's philosophies had formed his mind
and interwoven themselves into it and become
a part of its texture; he regarded himself as
Godwin's spiritual son.   Godwin was not without self-appreciation; indeed, it may be conjectured that from his point of view the last
syllable of his name was surplusage.   He lived
serene in his lofty world of philosophy, far
above the mean interests that absorbed smaller
men, and only came down to the ground at
intervals to pass the hat for alms to pay his
debts with, and insult the man that relieved
him.   Several of his principles were out of the
ordinary.   For example, he was opposed to
marriage.   He was not aware that his preach-
ings from this text were but theory and wind;

he supposed he was in earnest in imploring
people to live together without marrying, until
Shelley furnished him a working model of his
scheme and a practical example to analyze, by
applying the principle in his own family; the
matter took a different and surprising aspect
then.   The late Matthew Arnold said that the
main defect in Shelley's make-up was that he
was destitute of the sense of humor.   This
episode must have escaped Mr. Arnold's attention.

But we have said enough about the head of
the new paradise.   Mrs. Godwin is described
as being in several ways a terror; and even
when her soul was in repose she wore green
spectacles.   But I suspect that her main un-
attractiveness was born of the fact that she
wrote the letters that are out in the appendix-
basket in the back yard—letters which are
an outrage and wholly untrustworthy, for they
say some kind things about poor Harriet and
tell some disagreeable truths about her husband; and these things make the fabulist grit
his teeth a good deal.

Next we have Fanny Godwin — a Godwin
by courtesy only; she was Mrs. Godwin's natural daughter by a former friend.   She was
a sweet and winning girl, but she presently

wearied of the Godwin paradise, and poisoned herself.

Last in the list is Jane (or Claire, as she preferred to call herself) Clairmont, daughter of Mrs. Godwin by a former marriage. She was very young and pretty and accommodating, and always ready to do what she could to make things pleasant. After Shelley ran off with her part-sister Mary, she became the guest of the pair, and contributed a natural child to their nursery—Allegra. Lord Byron was the father.

We have named the several members and advantages of the new paradise in Skinner Street, with its crazy book-shop underneath. Shelley was all right now, this was a better place than the other; more variety anyway, and more different kinds of fragrance. One could turn out poetry here without any trouble at all.

The way the new love-match came about was this: Shelley told Mary all his aggravations and sorrows and griefs, and about the wet-nurse and the bonnet-shop and the surgeon and the carriage, and the sister-in-law that blocked the London game, and about Cornelia and her mamma, and how they had turned him out of the house after making so much of him; and how he had deserted Harriet and then Harriet had deserted him, and how the reconciliation was working along and Harriet getting her poem by heart; and still he was not happy, and Mary pitied him, for she had had trouble herself. But I am not satisfied with this. It reads too much like statistics. It lacks smoothness and grace, and is too earthy and business-like. It has the sordid look of a trades-union procession out on strike. That is not the right form for it. The book does it better; we will fall back on the book and have a cake-walk:

"It was easy to divine that some restless grief possessed him; Mary herself was not unlearned in the lore of pain. His generous zeal in her father's behalf, his spiritual sonship to Godwin, his reverence for her mother's memory, were guarantees with Mary of his excellence.* The new friends could not lack subjects of discourse, and underneath their words about Mary's mother, and 'Political Justice,' and 'Rights of Woman,' were two young hearts, each feeling towards the other, each perhaps unaware, trembling in the direction of the other. The desire to assuage the suffering of one whose happiness has grown precious to us may become a hunger of the spirit as keen as any

* What she was after was guarantees of his excellence. That he stood ready to desert his wife and child was one of them, apparently.

other, and this hunger now possessed Mary's heart;
when her eyes rested unseen on Shelley, it was with
a look full of the ardor of a 'soothing pity.'"

Yes, that is better and has more composure.
That is just the way it happened. He told
her about the wet-nurse, she told him about
political justice; he told her about the deadly sister-in-law, she told him about her mother;
he told her about the bonnet-shop, she mur-
mured back about the rights of woman; then
he assuaged her, then she assuaged him; then
he assuaged her some more, next she assuaged
him some more; then they both assuaged one
another simultaneously; and so they went on
by the hour assuaging and assuaging and assuaging, until at last what was the result?
They were in love. It will happen so every
time.

"He had married a woman who, as he now persuaded himself, had never truly loved him, who loved
only his fortune and his rank, and who proved her
selfishness by deserting him in his misery."

I think that that is not quite fair to Harriet. We have no certainty that she knew
Cornelia had turned him out of the house. He
went back to Cornelia, and Harriet may have
supposed that he was as happy with her as

ever. Still, it was judicious to begin to lay on the whitewash, for Shelley is going to need many a coat of it now, and the sooner the reader becomes used to the intrusion of the brush the sooner he will get reconciled to it and stop fretting about it.

After Shelley's (conjectured) visit to Harriet at Bath—8th of June to 18th—"it seems to have been arranged that Shelley should henceforth join the Skinner Street household each day at dinner."

Nothing could be handier than this; things will swim along now.

"Although now Shelley was coming to believe that his wedded union with Harriet was a thing of the past, he had not ceased to regard her with affectionate consideration; he wrote to her frequently, and kept her informed of his whereabouts."

We must not get impatient over these curious inharmoniousnesses and irreconcilabilities in Shelley's character. You can see by the biographer's attitude towards them that there is nothing objectionable about them. Shelley was doing his best to make two adoring young creatures happy: he was regarding the one with affectionate consideration by mail, and he was assuaging the other one at home.

"Unhappy Harriet, residing at Bath, had perhaps never desired that the breach between herself and her husband should be irreparable and complete."

I find no fault with that sentence except that the "perhaps" is not strictly warranted. It should have been left out.   In support—or shall we say extenuation?—of this opinion I submit that there is not sufficient evidence to warrant the uncertainty which it implies.   The only "evidence" offered that Harriet was hard and proud and standing out against a reconciliation is a poem—the poem in which Shelley beseeches her to "bid the remorseless feeling flee" and "pity" if she "cannot love." We have just that as "evidence," and out of its meagre materials the biographer builds a cobhouse of conjectures as big as the Coliseum; conjectures which convince him, the prosecuting attorney, but ought to fall far short of convincing any fair-minded jury.

Shelley's love-poems may be very good evidence, but we know well that they are "good for this day and train only."   We are able to believe that they spoke the truth for that one day, but we know by experience that they could not be depended on to speak it the next. That very supplication for a rewarming of Harriet's chilled love was followed so sudden-

6

ly by the poet's plunge into an adoring passion for Mary Godwin that if it had been a
check it would have lost its value before a lazy
person could have gotten to the bank with it.

Hardness, stubbornness, pride, vindictiveness
—these may sometimes reside in a young wife
and mother of nineteen, but they are not
charged against Harriet Shelley outside of
that poem, and one has no right to insert them
into her character on such shadowy " evidence"
as that.   Peacock knew Harriet well, and she
has a flexible and persuadable look, as painted
by him :

> " Her manners were good, and her whole aspect and
> demeanor such manifest emanations of pure and truth-
> ful nature that to be once in her company was to
> know her thoroughly.   She was fond of her husband,
> and accommodated herself in every way to his tastes.
> If they mixed in society, she adorned it ; if they lived
> in retirement, she was satisfied ; if they travelled, she
> enjoyed the change of scene."

" Perhaps " she had never desired that the
breach should be irreparable and complete.
The truth is, we do not even know that there
was any breach at all at this time.   We know
that the husband and wife went before the
altar and took a new oath on the 24th of
March to love and cherish each other until

death—and this may be regarded as a sort of reconciliation itself, and a wiping out of the old grudges. Then Harriet went away, and the sister-in-law removed herself from her society. That was in April. Shelley wrote his "appeal" in May, but the corresponding went right along afterwards. We have a right to doubt that the subject of it was a "reconciliation," or that Harriet had any suspicion that she needed to be reconciled and that her husband was trying to persuade her to it—as the biographer has sought to make us believe, with his Coliseum of conjectures built out of a waste-basket of poetry. For we have "evidence" now—not poetry and conjecture. When Shelley had been dining daily in the Skinner Street paradise fifteen days and continuing the love-match which was already a fortnight old twenty-five days earlier, he forgot to write Harriet; forgot it the next day and the next. During four days Harriet got no letter from him. Then her fright and anxiety rose to expression-heat, and she wrote a letter to Shelley's publisher which seems to reveal to us that Shelley's letters to her had been the customary affectionate letters of husband to wife, and had carried no appeals for reconciliation and had not needed to:

"BATH (postmark July 7, 1814).

"MY DEAR SIR,—You will greatly oblige me by giving the enclosed to Mr. Shelley. I would not trouble you, but it is now four days since I have heard from him, which to me is an age. Will you write by return of post and tell me what has become of him? as I always fancy something dreadful has happened if I do not hear from him. If you tell me that he is well I shall not come to London, but if I do not hear from you or him I shall certainly come, as I cannot endure this dreadful state of suspense. You are his friend and you can feel for me.

"I remain yours truly,

"H. S."

Even without Peacock's testimony that "her whole aspect and demeanor were manifest emanations of a pure and truthful nature," we should hold this to be a truthful letter, a sincere letter, a loving letter; it bears those marks; I think it is also the letter of a person accustomed to receiving letters from her husband frequently, and that they have been of a welcome and satisfactory sort, too, this long time back — ever since the solemn remarriage and reconciliation at the altar most likely.

The biographer follows Harriet's letter with a conjecture. He conjectures that she "would now gladly have retraced her steps." Which means that it is proven that she had steps to retrace — proven by the poem. Well, if the poem is better evidence than the letter, we must let it stand at that.

Then the biographer attacks Harriet Shelley's honor—by authority of random and unverified gossip scavengered from a group of people whose very names make a person shudder: Mary Godwin, mistress to Shelley; her part-sister, discarded mistress of Lord Byron; Godwin, the philosophical tramp, who gathers his share of it from a shadow—that is to say, from a person whom he shirks out of naming. Yet the biographer dignifies this sorry rubbish with the name of "evidence."

Nothing remotely resembling a distinct charge from a named person professing to know is offered among this precious "evidence."

1. "Shelley *believed*" so and so.

2. Byron's discarded mistress says that Shelley told Mary Godwin so and so, and *Mary* told *her*.

3. "Shelley said" so and so—and later "admitted over and over again that he had been in error."

4. The unspeakable Godwin "wrote to Mr. Baxter" that he knew so and so "from unquestionable authority"—name not furnished.

How any man in his right mind could bring
himself to defile the grave of a shamefully
abused and defenceless girl with these base-
less fabrications, this manufactured filth, is in-
conceivable.   How any man, in his right mind
or out of it, could sit down and coldly try to persuade anybody to believe it, or listen patiently
to it, or, indeed, do anything but scoff at it and
deride it, is astonishing.

The charge insinuated by these odious slan-
ders is one of the most difficult of all offences
to prove; it is also one which no man has a
right to mention even in a whisper about any
woman, living or dead, unless he knows it to be
true, and not even then unless he can also *prove*
it to be true.   There is no justification for the
abomination of putting this stuff in the book.

Against Harriet Shelley's good name there
is not one scrap of tarnishing evidence, and
not even a scrap of evil gossip, that comes
from a source that entitles it to a hearing.

On the credit side of the account we have
strong opinions from the people who knew her
best.   Peacock says:

"I feel it due to the memory of Harriet to state my
most decided conviction that her conduct as a wife
was as pure, as true, as absolutely faultless, as that of
any who for such conduct are held most in honor."

Thornton Hunt, who had picked and published slight flaws in Harriet's character, says, as regards this alleged large one:

"There is not a trace of evidence or a whisper of scandal against her before her voluntary departure from Shelley."

Trelawney says:

"I was assured by the evidence of the few friends who knew both Shelley and his wife — Hookham, Hogg, Peacock, and one of the Godwins—that Harriet was perfectly innocent of all offence."

What excuse was there for raking up a parcel of foul rumors from malicious and discredited sources and flinging them at this dead girl's head? Her very defencelessness should have been her protection. The fact that all letters to her or about her, with almost every scrap of her own writing, had been diligently mislaid, leaving her case destitute of a voice, while every pen-stroke which could help her husband's side had been as diligently preserved, should have excused her from being brought to trial. Her witnesses have all disappeared, yet we see her summoned in her grave-clothes to plead for the life of her character, without the help of an advocate, before a disqualified judge and a packed jury.

Harriet Shelley wrote her distressed letter on the 7th of July. On the 28th her husband ran away with Mary Godwin and her part-sister Claire to the Continent. He deserted his wife when her confinement was approaching. She bore him a child at the end of November, his mistress bore him another one something over two months later. The truants were back in London before either of these events occurred.

On one occasion, presently, Shelley was so pressed for money to support his mistress with that he went to his wife and got some money of his that was in her hands—twenty pounds. Yet the mistress was not moved to gratitude; for later, when the wife was troubled to meet her engagements, the mistress makes this entry in her diary:

"Harriet sends her creditors here; nasty woman. Now we shall have to change our lodgings."

The deserted wife bore the bitterness and obloquy of her situation two years and a quarter; then she gave up, and drowned herself. A month afterwards the body was found in the water. Three weeks later Shelley married his mistress.

I must here be allowed to italicize a re-

mark of the biographer's concerning Harriet
Shelley:

*"That no act of Shelley's during the two years which
immediately preceded her death tended to cause the rash
act which brought her life to its close seems certain."*

Yet her husband had deserted her and her
children, and was living with a concubine all
that time! Why should a person attempt to
write biography when the simplest facts have
no meaning to him? This book is littered
with as crass stupidities as that one—deductions by the page which bear no discoverable
kinship to their premises.

The biographer throws off that extraordinary remark without any perceptible disturb-
ance to his serenity; for he follows it with a
sentimental justification of Shelley's conduct
which has not a pang of conscience in it, but
is silky and smooth and undulating and pious
—a cake-walk with all the colored brethren at
their best. There may be people who can read
that page and keep their temper, but it is
doubtful.

Shelley's life has the one indelible blot upon
it, but is otherwise worshipfully noble and
beautiful. It even stands out indestructibly
gracious and lovely from the ruck of these dis-

astrous pages, in spite of the fact that they
expose and establish his responsibility for his
forsaken wife's pitiful fate—a responsibility
which he himself tacitly admits in a letter to
Eliza Westbrook, wherein he refers to his taking up with Mary Godwin as an act which
Eliza "might excusably regard as the cause
of her sister's ruin."

FENIMORE COOPER'S LITERARY OFFENCES

FENIMORE COOPER'S LITERARY OFFENCES

The Pathfinder and *The Deerslayer* stand at the head of Cooper's novels as artistic creations. There are others of his works which contain parts as perfect as are to be found in these, and scenes even more thrilling. Not one can be compared with either of them as a finished whole.

The defects in both of these tales are comparatively slight. They were pure works of art.—*Prof. Lounsbury.*

The five tales reveal an extraordinary fulness of invention.

. . . One of the very greatest characters in fiction, Natty Bumppo. . . .

The craft of the woodsman, the tricks of the trapper, all the delicate art of the forest, were familiar to Cooper from his youth up.—*Prof. Brander Matthews.*

Cooper is the greatest artist in the domain of romantic fiction yet produced by America. — *Wilkie Collins.*

IT seems to me that it was far from right for the Professor of English Literature in Yale, the Professor of English Literature in Columbia, and Wilkie Collins to deliver opinions on Cooper's literature without having read some of it. It would have been much more decorous to keep silent and let persons talk who have read Cooper.

Cooper's art has some defects. In one place in *Deerslayer*, and in the restricted space of two-thirds of a page, Cooper has scored 114 offences against literary art out of a possible 115. It breaks the record.

There are nineteen rules governing literary art in the domain of romantic fiction—some say twenty-two. In *Deerslayer* Cooper violated eighteen of them. These eighteen require:

1. That a tale shall accomplish something and arrive somewhere. But the *Deerslayer* tale accomplishes nothing and arrives in the air.

2. They require that the episodes of a tale shall be necessary parts of the tale, and shall help to develop it. But as the *Deerslayer* tale is not a tale, and accomplishes nothing and arrives nowhere, the episodes have no rightful place in the work, since there was nothing for them to develop.

3. They require that the personages in a tale shall be alive, except in the case of corpses,

and that always the reader shall be able to tell the corpses from the others. But this detail has often been overlooked in the *Deerslayer* tale.

4. They require that the personages in a tale, both dead and alive, shall exhibit a sufficient excuse for being there. But this detail also has been overlooked in the *Deerslayer* tale.

5. They require that when the personages of a tale deal in conversation, the talk shall sound like human talk, and be talk such as human beings would be likely to talk in the given circumstances, and have a discoverable meaning, also a discoverable purpose, and a show of relevancy, and remain in the neighborhood of the subject in hand, and be interesting to the reader, and help out the tale, and stop when the people cannot think of anything more to say. But this requirement has been ignored from the beginning of the *Deerslayer* tale to the end of it.

6. They require that when the author describes the character of a personage in his tale, the conduct and conversation of that personage shall justify said description. But this law gets little or no attention in the *Deerslayer* tale, as Natty Bumppo's case will amply prove.

7. They require that when a personage talks like an illustrated, gilt-edged, tree-calf, hand-tooled, seven-dollar Friendship's Offering in the beginning of a paragraph, he shall not talk like a negro minstrel in the end of it. But this rule is flung down and danced upon in the *Deerslayer* tale.

8. They require that crass stupidities shall not be played upon the reader as "the craft of the woodsman, the delicate art of the forest," by either the author or the people in the tale. But this rule is persistently violated in the *Deerslayer* tale.

9. They require that the personages of a tale shall confine themselves to possibilities and let miracles alone; or, if they venture a miracle, the author must so plausibly set it forth as to make it look possible and reasonable. But these rules are not respected in the *Deerslayer* tale.

10. They require that the author shall make the reader feel a deep interest in the personages of his tale and in their fate; and that he shall make the reader love the good people in the tale and hate the bad ones. But the reader of the *Deerslayer* tale dislikes the good people in it, is indifferent to the others, and wishes they would all get drowned together.

11. They require that the characters in a tale shall be so clearly defined that the reader can tell beforehand what each will do in a given emergency. But in the *Deerslayer* tale this rule is vacated.

In addition to these large rules there are some little ones. These require that the author shall

12. *Say* what he is proposing to say, not merely come near it.

13. Use the right word, not its second cousin.

14. Eschew surplusage.

15. Not omit necessary details.

16. Avoid slovenliness of form.

17. Use good grammar.

18. Employ a simple and straightforward style.

Even these seven are coldly and persistently violated in the *Deerslayer* tale.

Cooper's gift in the way of invention was not a rich endowment ; but such as it was he liked to work it, he was pleased with the effects, and indeed he did some quite sweet things with it. In his little box of stage properties he kept six or eight cunning devices, tricks, artifices for his savages and woodsmen to deceive and circumvent each other with,

7

and he was never so happy as when he was working these innocent things and seeing them go. A favorite one was to make a moccasined person tread in the tracks of the moccasined enemy, and thus hide his own trail. Cooper wore out barrels and barrels of moccasins in working that trick. Another stage-property that he pulled out of his box pretty frequently was his broken twig. He prized his broken twig above all the rest of his effects, and worked it the hardest. It is a restful chapter in any book of his when somebody doesn't step on a dry twig and alarm all the reds and whites for two hundred yards around. Every time a Cooper person is in peril, and absolute silence is worth four dollars a minute, he is sure to step on a dry twig. There may be a hundred handier things to step on, but that wouldn't satisfy Cooper. Cooper requires him to turn out and find a dry twig; and if he can't do it, go and borrow one. In fact, the Leather Stocking Series ought to have been called the Broken Twig Series.

I am sorry there is not room to put in a few dozen instances of the delicate art of the forest, as practised by Natty Bumppo and some of the other Cooperian experts. Perhaps we may venture two or three samples. Cooper was a sailor—a naval officer; yet he gravely tells us how a vessel, driving towards a lee shore in a gale, is steered for a particular spot by her skipper because he knows of an *undertow* there which will hold her back against the gale and save her. For just pure woodcraft, or sailorcraft, or whatever it is, isn't that neat? For several years Cooper was daily in the society of artillery, and he ought to have noticed that when a cannon-ball strikes the ground it either buries itself or skips a hundred feet or so; skips again a hundred feet or so—and so on, till it finally gets tired and rolls. Now in one place he loses some "females"—as he always calls women — in the edge of a wood near a plain at night in a fog, on purpose to give Bumppo a chance to show off the delicate art of the forest before the reader. These mislaid people are hunting for a fort. They hear a cannon-blast, and a cannon-ball presently comes rolling into the wood and stops at their feet. To the females this suggests nothing. The case is very different with the admirable Bumppo. I wish I may never know peace again if he doesn't strike out promptly and *follow the track* of that cannon-ball across the plain through the dense fog and find the fort. Isn't it a daisy? If Cooper had any real knowledge of Nature's ways of doing things, he had a most delicate art in concealing the fact. For instance: one of his acute Indian experts, Chingachgook (pronounced Chicago, I think), has lost the trail of a person he is tracking through the forest. Apparently that trail is hopelessly lost. Neither you nor I could ever have guessed out the way to find it. It was very different with Chicago. Chicago was not stumped for long. He turned a running stream out of its course, and there, in the slush in its old bed, were that person's moccasin - tracks. The current did not wash them away, as it would have done in all other like cases—no, even the eternal laws of Nature have to vacate when Cooper wants to put up a delicate job of woodcraft on the reader.

We must be a little wary when Brander Matthews tells us that Cooper's books " reveal an extraordinary fulness of invention." As a rule, I am quite willing to accept Brander Matthews's literary judgments and applaud his lucid and graceful phrasing of them; but that particular statement needs to be taken with a few tons of salt. Bless your heart, Cooper hadn't any more invention than a horse; and I don't mean a high-class horse, either; I mean a clothes-horse. It would be very difficult to find a really clever "situation" in Cooper's books, and still more difficult to find one of any kind which he has failed to render absurd by his handling of it. Look at the episodes of "the caves"; and at the celebrated scuffle between Maqua and those others on the table-land a few days later; and at Hurry Harry's queer water-transit from the castle to the ark; and at Deerslayer's halfhour with his first corpse; and at the quarrel between Hurry Harry and Deerslayer later; and at—but choose for yourself; you can't go amiss.

If Cooper had been an observer his inventive faculty would have worked better; not more interestingly, but more rationally, more plausibly. Cooper's proudest creations in the way of "situations" suffer noticeably from the absence of the observer's protecting gift. Cooper's eye was splendidly inaccurate. Cooper seldom saw anything correctly. He saw nearly all things as through a glass eye, darkly. Of course a man who cannot see the commonest little every-day matters accurately is working at a disadvantage when he is constructing a "situation." In the *Deerslayer* tale Cooper has a stream which is fifty feet wide where it flows out of a lake; it presently

narrows to twenty as it meanders along for no
given reason, and yet when a stream acts like
that it ought to be required to explain itself.
Fourteen pages later the width of the brook's
outlet from the lake has suddenly shrunk thirty
feet, and become "the narrowest part of the
stream." This shrinkage is not accounted for.
The stream has bends in it, a sure indication
that it has alluvial banks and cuts them; yet
these bends are only thirty and fifty feet long.
If Cooper had been a nice and punctilious observer he would have noticed that the bends
were oftener nine hundred feet long than short
of it.

Cooper made the exit of that stream fifty
feet wide, in the first place, for no particular
reason; in the second place, he narrowed it to
less than twenty to accommodate some Indians. He bends a "sapling" to the form of
an arch over this narrow passage, and conceals
six Indians in its foliage. They are "laying"
for a settler's scow or ark which is coming up
the stream on its way to the lake; it is being
hauled against the stiff current by a rope
whose stationary end is anchored in the lake;
its rate of progress cannot be more than a
mile an hour. Cooper describes the ark, but
pretty obscurely. In the matter of dimen-

sions " it was little more than a modern canal-boat." Let us guess, then, that it was about one hundred and forty feet long. It was of " greater breadth than common." Let us guess, then, that it was about sixteen feet wide. This leviathan had been prowling down bends which were but a third as long as itself, and scraping between banks where it had only two feet of space to spare on each side. We cannot too much admire this miracle. A low-roofed log dwelling occupies "two-thirds of the ark's length"—a dwelling ninety feet long and sixteen feet wide, let us say—a kind of vestibule train. The dwelling has two rooms—each forty-five feet long and sixteen feet wide, let us guess. One of them is the bedroom of the Hutter girls, Judith and Hetty; the other is the parlor in the daytime, at night it is papa's bedchamber. The ark is arriving at the stream's exit now, whose width has been reduced to less than twenty feet to accommodate the Indians—say to eighteen. There is a foot to spare on each side of the boat. Did the Indians notice that there was going to be a tight squeeze there? Did they notice that they could make money by climbing down out of that arched sapling and just stepping aboard when the ark scraped by? No; other Indians would have noticed these things, but Cooper's Indians never notice anything. Cooper thinks they are marvellous creatures for noticing, but he was almost always in error about his Indians. There was seldom a sane one among them.

The ark is one hundred and forty feet long; the dwelling is ninety feet long. The idea of the Indians is to drop softly and secretly from the arched sapling to the dwelling as the ark creeps along under it at the rate of a mile an hour, and butcher the family. It will take the ark a minute and a half to pass under. It will take the ninety foot dwelling a minute to pass under. Now, then, what did the six Indians do? It would take you thirty years to guess, and even then you would have to give it up, I believe. Therefore, I will tell you what the Indians did. Their chief, a person of quite extraordinary intellect for a Cooper Indian, warily watched the canal-boat as it squeezed along under him, and when he had got his calculations fined down to exactly the right shade, as he judged, he let go and dropped. And *missed the house!* That is actually what he did. He missed the house, and landed in the stern of the scow. It was not much of a fall, yet it knocked him silly. He lay there unconscious. If the house had been ninety-seven feet long he would have made the trip. The fault was Cooper's, not his. The error lay in the construction of the house. Cooper was no architect.

There still remained in the roost five Indians. The boat has passed under and is now out of their reach. Let me explain what the five did—you would not be able to reason it out for yourself. No. 1 jumped for the boat, but fell in the water astern of it. Then No. 2 jumped for the boat, but fell in the water still farther astern of it. Then No. 3 jumped for the boat, and fell a good way astern of it. Then No. 4 jumped for the boat, and fell in the water *away* astern. Then even No. 5 made a jump for the boat—for he was a Cooper Indian. In the matter of intellect, the difference between a Cooper Indian and the Indian that stands in front of the cigar-shop is not spacious. The scow episode is really a sublime burst of invention; but it does not thrill, because the inaccuracy of the details throws a sort of air of fictitiousness and general improbability over it. This comes of Cooper's inadequacy as an observer.

The reader will find some examples of Cooper's high talent for inaccurate observation in the account of the shooting - match in *The Pathfinder*.

> "A common wrought nail was driven lightly into the target, its head having been first touched with paint."

The color of the paint is not stated—an important omission, but Cooper deals freely in important omissions.   No, after all, it was not an important omission; for this nail-head is *a hundred yards* from the marksmen, and could not be seen by them at that distance, no matter what its color might be.   How far can the best eyes see a common house-fly?   A hundred yards? It is quite impossible.   Very well; eyes that cannot see a house-fly that is a hundred yards away cannot see an ordinary nail-head at that distance, for the size of the two objects is the same.   It takes a keen eye to see a fly or a nail-head at fifty yards—one hundred and fifty feet.   Can the reader do it?

The nail was lightly driven, its head painted, and game called.   Then the Cooper miracles began.   The bullet of the first marksman chipped an edge of the nail-head; the next man's bullet drove the nail a little way into the target—and removed all the paint.   Haven't the miracles gone far enough now?   Not to

suit Cooper; for the purpose of this whole
scheme is to show off his prodigy, Deerslayer-
Hawkeye-Long-Rifle-Leather-Stocking-Path-
finder-Bumppo before the ladies.

"'Be all ready to clench it, boys!' cried out Pathfinder, stepping into his friend's tracks the instant
they were vacant. 'Never mind a new nail; I can
see that, though the paint is gone, and what I can see
I can hit at a hundred yards, though it were only a
mosquito's eye. Be ready to clench!'

"The rifle cracked, the bullet sped its way, and the
head of the nail was buried in the wood, covered by
the piece of flattened lead."

There, you see, is a man who could hunt
flies with a rifle, and command a ducal salary
in a Wild West show to-day if we had him
back with us.

The recorded feat is certainly surprising
just as it stands; but it is not surprising
enough for Cooper. Cooper adds a touch.
He has made Pathfinder do this miracle with
another man's rifle; and not only that, but
Pathfinder did not have even the advantage
of loading it himself. He had everything
against him, and yet he made that impossible
shot; and not only made it, but did it with absolute confidence, saying, "Be ready to clench."
Now a person like that would have undertaken

that same feat with a brickbat, and with Cooper to help he would have achieved it, too.

Pathfinder showed off handsomely that day before the ladies. His very first feat was a thing which no Wild West show can touch. He was standing with the group of marksmen, observing—a hundred yards from the target, mind; one Jasper raised his rifle and drove the centre of the bull's-eye. Then the Quartermaster fired. The target exhibited no result this time. There was a laugh. "It's a dead miss," said Major Lundie. Pathfinder waited an impressive moment or two; then said, in that calm, indifferent, know-it-all way of his, "No, Major, he has covered Jasper's bullet, as will be seen if any one will take the trouble to examine the target."

Wasn't it remarkable! How *could* he see that little pellet fly through the air and enter that distant bullet-hole? Yet that is what he did; for nothing is impossible to a Cooper person. Did any of those people have any deep-seated doubts about this thing? No; for that would imply sanity, and these were all Cooper people.

"The respect for Pathfinder's skill and for his *quickness and accuracy of sight*" (the italics are mine) "was so profound and general, that the instant he made this declaration the spectators began to distrust their own opinions, and a dozen rushed to the target in order to ascertain the fact. There, sure enough, it was found that the Quartermaster's bullet had gone through the hole made by Jasper's, and that, too, so accurately as to require a minute examination to be certain of the circumstance, which, however, was soon clearly established by discovering one bullet over the other in the stump against which the target was placed."

They made a " minute " examination ; but never mind, how could they know that there were two bullets in that hole without digging the latest one out? for neither probe nor eyesight could prove the presence of any more than one bullet. Did they dig? No; as we shall see. It is the Pathfinder's turn now; he steps out before the ladies, takes aim, and fires.

But, alas! here is a disappointment; an incredible, an unimaginable disappointment — for the target's aspect is unchanged; there is nothing there but that same old bullet-hole!

" ' If one dared to hint at such a thing,' cried Major Duncan, ' I should say that the Pathfinder has also missed the target !' "

As nobody had missed it yet, the " also " was not necessary; but never mind about that, for the Pathfinder is going to speak.

"'No, no, Major,' said he, confidently, 'that *would* be a risky declaration. I didn't load the piece, and can't say what was in it; but if it was lead, you will find the bullet driving down those of the Quartermaster and Jasper, else is not my name Pathfinder.'

"A shout from the target announced the truth of this assertion."

Is the miracle sufficient as it stands? Not for Cooper. The Pathfinder speaks again, as he "now slowly advances towards the stage occupied by the females":

"'That's not all, boys, that's not all; if you find the target touched at all, I'll own to a miss. The Quartermaster cut the wood, but you'll find no wood cut by that last messenger.'"

The miracle is at last complete. He knew —doubtless *saw*—at the distance of a hundred yards —that his bullet had passed into the hole *without fraying the edges*. There were now three bullets in that one hole—three bullets embedded processionally in the body of the stump back of the target. Everybody knew this—somehow or other—and yet nobody had dug any of them out to make sure. Cooper is not a close observer, but he is interesting. He is certainly always that, no matter what happens. And he is more interesting when he is not noticing what he is about than when he is. This is a considerable merit.

The conversations in the Cooper books have a curious sound in our modern ears. To believe that such talk really ever came out of people's mouths would be to believe that there was a time when time was of no value to a person who thought he had something to say; when it was the custom to spread a two-minute remark out to ten; when a man's mouth was a rolling-mill, and busied itself all day long in turning four-foot pigs of thought into thirty-foot bars of conversational railroad iron by attenuation; when subjects were seldom faithfully stuck to, but the talk wandered all around and arrived nowhere; when conversations consisted mainly of irrelevances, with here and there a relevancy, a relevancy with an embarrassed look, as not being able to explain how it got there.

Cooper was certainly not a master in the construction of dialogue. Inaccurate observation defeated him here as it defeated him in so many other enterprises of his. He even failed to notice that the man who talks corrupt English six days in the week must and will talk it on the seventh, and can't help himself. In the *Deerslayer* story he lets Deerslayer talk the showiest kind of book talk sometimes, and at other times the basest of base dialects. For instance, when some one asks him if he has a sweetheart, and if so, where she abides, this is his majestic answer:

"'She's in the forest—hanging from the boughs of the trees, in a soft rain—in the dew on the open grass—the clouds that float about in the blue heavens —the birds that sing in the woods—the sweet springs where I slake my thirst—and in all the other glorious gifts that come from God's Providence!'"

And he preceded that, a little before, with this:

"'It consarns me as all things that touches a fri'nd consarns a fri'nd.'"

And this is another of his remarks:

"'If I was Injin born, now, I might tell of this, or carry in the scalp and boast of the expl'ite afore the whole tribe; or if my inimy had only been a bear'"— and so on.

We cannot imagine such a thing as a veteran Scotch Commander-in-Chief comporting himself in the field like a windy melodramatic actor, but Cooper could. On one occasion Alice and Cora were being chased by the French through a fog in the neighborhood of their father's fort:

"'*Point de quartier aux coquins!*' cried an eager pursuer, who seemed to direct the operations of the enemy.

"' Stand firm and be ready, my gallant 6oths!' suddenly exclaimed a voice above them ; 'wait to see the enemy ; fire low, and sweep the glacis.'

"' Father ! father !' exclaimed a piercing cry from out the mist; 'it is I! Alice ! thy own Elsie ! spare, O ! save your daughters !'

"' Hold !' shouted the former speaker, in the awful tones of parental agony, the sound reaching even to the woods, and rolling back in solemn echo. ' 'Tis she ! God has restored me my children ! Throw open the sally-port; to the field, 6oths, to the field; pull not a trigger, lest ye kill my lambs ! Drive off these dogs of France with your steel.' "

Cooper's word-sense was singularly dull. When a person has a poor ear for music he will flat and sharp right along without knowing it. He keeps near the tune, but it is *not* the tune. When a person has a poor ear for words, the result is a literary flatting and sharping ; you perceive what he is intending to say, but you also perceive that he doesn't *say* it. This is Cooper. He was not a word-musician. His ear was satisfied with the *approximate* word. I will furnish some circumstantial evidence in support of this charge. My instances are gathered from half a dozen

8

pages of the tale called *Deerslayer*. He uses
"verbal," for "oral"; "precision," for "facility"; "phenomena," for "marvels"; "necessary," for "predetermined"; "unsophisticated,"
for "primitive"; "preparation," for "expect-
ancy"; "rebuked," for "subdued"; "depend-
ant on," for "resulting from"; "fact," for
"condition"; "fact," for "conjecture"; "pre-
caution," for "caution"; "explain," for "de-
termine"; "mortified," for "disappointed";
"meretricious," for "factitious"; "materially,"
for "considerably"; "decreasing," for "deep-
ening"; "increasing," for "disappearing";
"embedded," for "enclosed"; "treacherous,"
for "hostile"; "stood," for "stooped"; "softened," for "replaced"; "rejoined," for "remarked"; "situation," for "condition"; "different," for "differing"; "insensible," for
"unsentient"; "brevity," for "celerity"; "dis-
trusted," for "suspicious"; "mental imbecility," for "imbecility"; "eyes," for "sight";
"counteracting," for "opposing"; "funeral
obsequies," for "obsequies."

There have been daring people in the world
who claimed that Cooper could write English, but they are all dead now—all dead but
Lounsbury. I don't remember that Lounsbury makes the claim in so many words, still

he makes it, for he says that *Deerslayer* is a
"pure work of art." Pure, in that connection, means faultless—faultless in all details—
and language is a detail. If Mr. Lounsbury
had only compared Cooper's English with the
English which he writes himself — but it is
plain that he didn't; and so it is likely that he
imagines until this day that Cooper's is as
clean and compact as his own. Now I feel
sure, deep down in my heart, that Cooper
wrote about the poorest English that exists in
our language, and that the English of *Deerslayer* is the very worst that even Cooper ever
wrote.

I may be mistaken, but it does seem to me
that *Deerslayer* is not a work of art in any
sense; it does seem to me that it is destitute
of every detail that goes to the making of a
work of art; in truth, it seems to me that
Deerslayer is just simply a literary *delirium
tremens*.

A work of art? It has no invention; it has
no order, system, sequence, or result; it has
no lifelikeness, no thrill, no stir, no seeming of
reality; its characters are confusedly drawn,
and by their acts and words they prove that
they are not the sort of people the author
claims that they are; its humor is pathetic;

its pathos is funny; its conversations are—oh! indescribable; its love-scenes odious; its English a crime against the language.

Counting these out, what is left is Art. I think we must all admit that.

TRAVELLING WITH A REFORMER

TRAVELLING WITH A REFORMER

LAST spring I went out to Chicago to see
the Fair, and although I did not see it my
trip was not wholly lost—there were compen-
sations. In New York I was introduced to a
major in the regular army who said he was
going to the Fair, and we agreed to go together. I had to go to Boston first, but that
did not interfere ; he said he would go along,
and put in the time. He was a handsome
man, and built like a gladiator. But his ways
were gentle, and his speech was soft and per-
suasive. He was companionable, but exceedingly reposeful. Yes, and wholly destitute of
the sense of humor. He was full of interest
in everything that went on around him, but
his serenity was indestructible ; nothing disturbed him, nothing excited him.

But before the day was done I found that
deep down in him somewhere he had a passion, quiet as he was—a passion for reforming
petty public abuses. He stood for citizenship

—it was his hobby.   His idea was that every
citizen of the republic ought to consider himself an unofficial policeman, and keep unsala-
ried watch and ward over the laws and their
execution.   He thought that the only effective way of preserving and protecting public
rights was for each citizen to do his share in
preventing or punishing such infringements
of them as came under his personal notice.

It was a good scheme, but I thought it
would keep a body in trouble all the time ; it
seemed to me that one would be always trying
to get offending little officials discharged, and
perhaps getting laughed at for all reward.   But
he said no, I had the wrong idea; that there
was no occasion to get anybody discharged ;
that in fact you *mustn't* get anybody discharged ; that that would itself be a failure ;
no, one must reform the man—reform him and
make him useful where he was.

" Must one report the offender and then beg
his superior not to discharge him, but repri-
mand him and keep him ?"

" No, that is not the idea ; you don't report
him at all, for then you risk his bread and but-
ter.   You can act as if you are *going* to report
him — when nothing else will answer.   But
that's an extreme case.   That is a sort of

force, and force is bad. Diplomacy is the effective thing. Now if a man has tact—if a man will exercise diplomacy—"

For two minutes we had been standing at a telegraph wicket, and during all this time the Major had been trying to get the attention of one of the young operators, but they were all busy skylarking. The Major spoke now, and asked one of them to take his telegram. He got for reply:

"I reckon you can wait a minute, can't you?" and the skylarking went on.

The Major said yes, he was not in a hurry. Then he wrote another telegram:

"*President Western Union Tel. Co.:*

"Come and dine with me this evening. I can tell you how business is conducted in one of your branches."

Presently the young fellow who had spoken so pertly a little before reached out and took the telegram, and when he read it he lost color and began to apologize and explain. He said he would lose his place if this deadly telegram was sent, and he might never get another. If he could be let off this time he would give no cause of complaint again. The compromise was accepted.

As we walked away, the Major said:

"Now, you see, that was diplomacy — and you see how it worked. It wouldn't do any good to bluster, the way people are always doing — that boy can always give you as good as you send, and you'll come out defeated and ashamed of yourself pretty nearly always. But you see he stands no chance against diplomacy. Gentle words and diplomacy—those are the tools to work with."

"Yes, I see; but everybody wouldn't have had your opportunity. It isn't everybody that is on those familiar terms with the president of the Western Union."

"Oh, you misunderstand. I don't know the president—I only use him diplomatically. It is for his good and for the public good. There's no harm in it."

I said, with hesitation and diffidence:

"But is it ever right or noble to tell a lie?"

He took no note of the delicate self-righteousness of the question, but answered, with undisturbed gravity and simplicity:

"Yes, sometimes. Lies told to injure a person, and lies told to profit yourself are not justifiable, but lies told to help another person, and lies told in the public interest—oh, well, that is quite another matter. Anybody knows

that. But never mind about the methods:
you see the result. That youth is going to be
useful now, and well-behaved. He had a good
face. He was worth saving. Why, he was
worth saving on his mother's account if not
his own. Of course, he has a mother—sisters,
too. Damn these people who are always forgetting that! Do you know, I've never fought
a duel in my life—never once—and yet have
been challenged, like other people. I could
always see the other man's unoffending wom-
en folks or his little children standing between him and me. *They* hadn't done anything — I couldn't break *their* hearts, you
know."

He corrected a good many little abuses in
the course of the day, and always without
friction—always with a fine and dainty " diplomacy" which left no sting behind ; and he got
such happiness and such contentment out of
these performances that I was obliged to envy
him his trade—and perhaps would have adopt-
ed it if I could have managed the necessary
deflections from fact as confidently with my
mouth as I believe I could with a pen, behind
the shelter of print, after a little practice.

Away late that night we were coming up-
town in a horse-car when three boisterous

roughs got aboard, and began to fling hilarious obscenities and profanities right and left
among the timid passengers, some of whom
were women and children. Nobody resisted
or retorted; the conductor tried soothing
words and moral suasion, but the roughs only
called him names and laughed at him. Very
soon I saw that the Major realized that this
was a matter which was in his line; evidently
he was turning over his stock of diplomacy in
his mind and getting ready. I felt that the
first diplomatic remark he made in this place
would bring down a land-slide of ridicule upon
him and maybe something worse; but before
I could whisper to him and check him he had
begun, and it was too late. He said, in a level
and dispassionate tone:

"Conductor, you must put these swine out.
I will help you."

I was not looking for that. In a flash the
three roughs plunged at him. But none of
them arrived. He delivered three such blows
as one could not expect to encounter outside
the prize-ring, and neither of the men had life
enough left in him to get up from where he
fell. The Major dragged them out and threw
them off the car, and we got under way again.

I was astonished; astonished to see a lamb

act so; astonished at the strength displayed, and the clean and comprehensive result; astonished at the brisk and business-like style of the whole thing. The situation had a humorous side to it, considering how much I had been hearing about mild persuasion and gentle diplomacy all day from this pile-driver, and I would have liked to call his attention to that feature and do some sarcasms about it; but when I looked at him I saw that it would be of no use—his placid and contented face had no ray of humor in it; he would not have understood. When we left the car, I said:

"That was a good stroke of diplomacy — three good strokes of diplomacy, in fact."

"*That?* That wasn't diplomacy. You are quite in the wrong. Diplomacy is a wholly different thing. One cannot apply it to that sort, they would not understand it. No, that was not diplomacy; it was force."

"Now that you mention it, I—yes, I think perhaps you are right."

"Right? Of course I am right. It was just force."

"I think, myself, it had the outside aspect of it. Do you often have to reform people in that way?"

"Far from it. It hardly ever happens. Not

oftener than once in half a year, at the outside."

"Those men will get well?"

"Get well? Why, certainly they will. They
are not in any danger. I know how to hit
and where to hit. You noticed that I did not
hit them under the jaw. That would have
killed them."

I believed that. I remarked—rather wittily,
as I thought — that he had been a lamb all
day, but now had all of a sudden developed
into a ram—battering-ram; but with dulcet
frankness and simplicity he said no, a battering-ram was quite a different thing and not in
use now. This was maddening, and I came
near bursting out and saying he had no more
appreciation of wit than a jackass—in fact, I
had it right on my tongue, but did not say
it, knowing there was no hurry and I could
say it just as well some other time over the
telephone.

We started to Boston the next afternoon.
The smoking-compartment in the parlor-car
was full, and we went into the regular smoker.
Across the aisle in the front seat sat a meek,
farmer-looking old man with a sickly pallor in
his face, and he was holding the door open
with his foot to get the air. Presently a big

brakeman came rushing through, and when he
got to the door he stopped, gave the farmer
an ugly scowl, then wrenched the door to with
such energy as to almost snatch the old man's
boot off.   Then on he plunged about his business.   Several passengers laughed, and the
old gentleman looked pathetically shamed and
grieved.

After a little the conductor passed along, and
the Major stopped him and asked him a question in his habitually courteous way:

"Conductor, where does one report the mis-
conduct of a brakeman?   Does one report to
you?"

"You can report him at New Haven if you
want to.   What has he been doing?"

The Major told the story.   The conductor
seemed amused.   He said, with just a touch
of sarcasm in his bland tones:

"As I understand you, the brakeman didn't
say anything."

"No, he didn't say anything."

"But he scowled, you say."

"Yes."

"And snatched the door loose in a rough
way."

"Yes."

"That's the whole business, is it?"

"Yes, that is the whole of it."

The conductor smiled pleasantly, and said:

"Well, if you want to report him, all right, but I don't quite make out what it's going to amount to. You'll say—as I understand you—that the brakeman insulted this old gentleman. They'll ask you what he *said*. You'll say he didn't say anything at all. I reckon they'll say, how are you going to make out an insult when you acknowledge yourself that he didn't say a word."

There was a murmur of applause at the conductor's compact reasoning, and it gave him pleasure—you could see it in his face. But the Major was not disturbed. He said:

"There—now you have touched upon a crying defect in the complaint-system. The railway officials—as the public think and as you also seem to think—are not aware that there are any kind of insults except *spoken* ones. So nobody goes to headquarters and reports insults of manner, insults of gesture, look, and so forth; and yet these are sometimes harder to bear than any words. They are bitter hard to bear because there is nothing tangible to take hold of; and the insulter can always say, if called before the railway officials, that he never dreamed of intending any offence. It

seems to me that the officials ought to special-
ly and urgently request the public to report
unworded affronts and incivilities."

The conductor laughed, and said :

"Well, that *would* be trimming it pretty
fine, sure !"

"But not too fine, I think.   I will report
this matter at New Haven, and I have an idea
that I'll be thanked for it."

The conductor's face lost something of its
complacency; in fact, it settled to a quite sober
cast as the owner of it moved away.   I said :

"You are not really going to bother with
that trifle, are you ?"

"It isn't a trifle.   Such things ought always
to be reported.   It is a public duty, and no
citizen has a right to shirk it.   But I sha'n't
have to report this case."

"Why ?"

"It won't be necessary.   Diplomacy will do
the business.   You'll see."

Presently the conductor came on his rounds
again, and when he reached the Major he leaned
over and said :

"That's all right.   You needn't report him.
He's responsible to me, and if he does it again
I'll give him a talking to."

The Major's response was cordial :

9

"Now that is what I like! You mustn't think that I was moved by any vengeful spirit, for that wasn't the case. It was duty—just a sense of duty, that was all. My brother-in-law is one of the directors of the road, and when he learns that you are going to reason with your brakeman the very next time he brutally insults an unoffending old man it will please him, you may be sure of that."

The conductor did not look as joyous as one might have thought he would, but on the contrary looked sickly and uncomfortable. He stood around a little; then said:

"*I* think something ought to be done to him *now*. I'll discharge him."

"Discharge him? What good would that do? Don't you think it would be better wisdom to teach him better ways and keep him?"

"Well, there's something in that. What would you suggest?"

"He insulted the old gentleman in presence of all these people. How would it do to have him come and apologize in their presence?"

"I'll have him here right off. And I want to say this: If people would do as you've done, and report such things to me instead of keeping mum and going off and blackguarding the

road, you'd see a different state of things pretty soon. I'm much obliged to you."

The brakeman came and apologized. After
he was gone the Major said:

"Now, you see how simple and easy that
was. The ordinary citizen would have accomplished nothing—the brother-in-law of a director can accomplish anything he wants to."

"But are you really the brother-in-law of a
director?"

"Always. Always when the public interests require it. I have a brother-in-law on all
the boards—everywhere. It saves me a world
of trouble."

"It is a good wide relationship."

"Yes. I have over three hundred of them."

"Is the relationship never doubted by a
conductor?"

"I have never met with a case. It is the
honest truth—I never have."

"Why didn't you let him go ahead and discharge the brakeman, in spite of your favorite
policy? You know he deserved it."

The Major answered with something which
really had a sort of distant resemblance to impatience:

"If you would stop and think a moment
you wouldn't ask such a question as that. Is

a brakeman a dog, that nothing but dog's methods will do for him? He is a man, and has a man's fight for life. And he always has a sister, or a mother, or wife and children to support. Always—there are no exceptions. When you take his living away from him you take theirs away too—and what have they done to you? Nothing. And where is the profit in discharging an uncourteous brakeman and hiring another just like him? It's unwisdom. Don't you see that the rational thing to do is to *reform* the brakeman and keep him? Of course it is."

Then he quoted with admiration the conduct of a certain division superintendent of the Consolidated road, in a case where a switchman of two years' experience was negligent once and threw a train off the track and killed several people. Citizens came in a passion to urge the man's dismissal, but the superintendent said:

"No, you are wrong. He has learned his lesson, he will throw no more trains off the track. He is twice as valuable as he was before. I shall keep him."

We had only one more adventure on the trip. Between Hartford and Springfield the train-boy came shouting in with an armful of literature and dropped a sample into a slumbering gentleman's lap, and the man woke up with a start. He was very angry, and he and a couple of friends discussed the outrage with much heat. They sent for the parlor-car conductor and described the matter, and were determined to have the boy expelled from his situation. The three complainants were wealthy Holyoke merchants, and it was evident that the conductor stood in some awe of them. He tried to pacify them, and explained that the boy was not under his authority, but under that of one of the news companies; but he accomplished nothing.

Then the Major volunteered some testimony for the defence. He said:

"I saw it all. You gentlemen have not meant to exaggerate the circumstances, but still that is what you have done. The boy has done nothing more than all train-boys do. If you want to get his ways softened down and his manners reformed, I am with you and ready to help, but it isn't fair to get him discharged without giving him a chance."

But they were angry, and would hear of no compromise. They were well acquainted with the president of the Boston & Albany, they said, and would put everything aside

next day and go up to Boston and fix that
boy.

The Major said he would be on hand too,
and would do what he could to save the boy.
One of the gentlemen looked him over, and
said:

"Apparently it is going to be a matter of
who can wield the most influence with the
president. Do you know Mr. Bliss personally?"

The Major said, with composure:

"Yes; he is my uncle."

The effect was satisfactory. There was an
awkward silence for a minute or more; then
the hedging and the half-confessions of over-
haste and exaggerated resentment began, and
soon everything was smooth and friendly and
sociable, and it was resolved to drop the matter and leave the boy's bread-and-butter un-
molested.

It turned out as I had expected: the president of the road was not the Major's uncle at
all—except by adoption, and for this day and
train only.

We got into no episodes on the return journey. Probably it was because we took a night
train and slept all the way.

We left New York Saturday night by the
Pennsylvania road. After breakfast the next

morning we went into the parlor-car, but found it a dull place and dreary. There were but few people in it and nothing going on. Then we went into the little smoking-compartment of the same car and found three gentlemen in there. Two of them were grumbling over one of the rules of the road—a rule which forbade card-playing on the trains on Sunday. They had started an innocent game of high-low-jack and been stopped. The Major was interested. He said to the third gentleman:

"Did you object to the game?"

"Not at all. I am a Yale professor and a religious man, but my prejudices are not extensive."

Then the Major said to the others:

"You are at perfect liberty to resume your game, gentlemen; no one here objects."

One of them declined the risk, but the other one said he would like to begin again if the Major would join him. So they spread an overcoat over their knees and the game proceeded. Pretty soon the parlor-car conductor arrived, and said, brusquely:

"There, there, gentlemen, that won't do. Put up the cards—it's not allowed."

The Major was shuffling. He continued to shuffle, and said:

" By whose order is it forbidden ?"

" It's my order.   I forbid it."

The dealing began.   The Major asked:

" Did you invent the idea ?"

" What idea ?"

" The idea of forbidding card-playing on Sunday."

" No—of course not."

" Who did ?"

" The company."

" Then it isn't your order, after all, but the company's.   Is that it ?"

" Yes.   But you don't stop playing ; I have to require you to stop playing immediately."

" Nothing is gained by hurry, and often much is lost.   Who authorized the company to issue such an order ?"

" My dear sir, that is a matter of no consequence to me, and—"

" But you forget that you are not the only person concerned.   It may be a matter of consequence to me.   It is indeed a matter of very great importance to me.   I cannot violate a legal requirement of my country without dishonoring myself ; I cannot allow any man or corporation to hamper my liberties with illegal rules—a thing which railway companies are always trying to do—without dishonoring my citizenship. So I come back to that question: By whose authority has the company issued this order?"

"I don't *know.* That's *their* affair."

"Mine, too. I doubt if the company has any right to issue such a rule. This road runs through several States. Do you know what State we are in now, and what its laws are in matters of this kind?"

"Its laws do not concern me, but the company's orders do. It is my duty to stop this game, gentlemen, and it *must* be stopped."

"Possibly; but still there is no hurry. In hotels they post certain rules in the rooms, but they always quote passages from the State law as authority for these requirements. I see nothing posted here of this sort. Please produce your authority and let us arrive at a decision, for you see yourself that you are marring the game."

"I have nothing of the kind, but I have my orders, and that is sufficient. They must be obeyed."

"Let us not jump to conclusions. It will be better all around to examine into the matter without heat or haste, and see just where we stand before either of us makes a mistake —for the curtailing of the liberties of a citizen of the United States is a much more serious matter than you and the railroads seem to think, and it cannot be done in my person until the curtailer proves his right to do so. Now—"

"My dear sir, *will* you put down those cards?"

"All in good time, perhaps. It depends. You say this order must be obeyed. *Must.* It is a strong word. You see yourself how strong it is. A wise company would not arm you with so drastic an order as this, of *course*, without appointing a penalty for its infringement. Otherwise it runs the risk of being a dead letter and a thing to laugh at. What is the appointed penalty for an infringement of this law?"

"Penalty? I never heard of any."

"Unquestionably you must be mistaken. Your company orders you to come here and rudely break up an innocent amusement, and furnishes you no way to enforce the order? Don't you see that that is nonsense? What do you *do* when people refuse to obey this order? Do you take the cards away from them?"

"No."

"Do you put the offender off at the next station?"

"Well, no—of course we couldn't if he had a ticket."

"Do you have him up before a court?"

The conductor was silent and apparently troubled. The Major started a new deal, and said:

"You see that you are helpless, and that the company has placed you in a foolish position. You are furnished with an arrogant order, and you deliver it in a blustering way, and when you come to look into the matter you find you haven't any way of enforcing obedience."

The conductor said, with chill dignity:

"Gentlemen, you have heard the order, and my duty is ended. As to obeying it or not, you will do as you think fit." And he turned to leave.

"But wait. The matter is not yet finished. I think you are mistaken about your duty being ended; but if it really is, I myself have a duty to perform yet."

"How do you mean?"

"Are you going to report my disobedience at headquarters in Pittsburg?"

"No. What good would that do?"

"You must report me, or I will report you."

"Report me for what?"

"For disobeying the company's orders in not stopping this game. As a citizen it is my duty to help the railway companies keep their servants to their work."

"Are you in earnest?"

"Yes, I am in earnest. I have nothing against you as a man, but I have this against you as an officer—that you have not carried out that order, and if you do not report me I must report you. And I will."

The conductor looked puzzled, and was thoughtful a moment; then he burst out with:

"I seem to be getting *myself* into a scrape! It's all a muddle; I can't make head or tail of it; it's never happened before; they always knocked under and never said a word, and so *I* never saw how ridiculous that stupid order with no penalty is. *I* don't want to report anybody, and I don't want to *be* reported— why, it might do me no end of harm! Now *do* go on with the game—play the whole day if you want to—and don't let's have any more trouble about it!"

"No, I only sat down here to establish this gentleman's rights — he can have his place now. But before you go won't you tell me what you think the company made this rule for? Can you imagine an excuse for it? I mean a rational one—an excuse that is not on its face silly, and the invention of an idiot?"

"Why, surely I can. The reason it was made is plain enough. It is to save the feelings of the other passengers—the religious ones among them, I mean. They would not like it, to have the Sabbath desecrated by card-playing on the train."

"I just thought as much. They are willing to desecrate it themselves by travelling on Sunday, but they are not willing that other people—"

"By gracious, you've hit it! I never thought of that before. The fact is, it *is* a silly rule when you come to look into it."

At this point the train-conductor arrived, and was going to shut down the game in a very high-handed fashion, but the parlor-car conductor stopped him and took him aside to explain. Nothing more was heard of the matter.

I was ill in bed eleven days in Chicago and got no glimpse of the Fair, for I was obliged to return east as soon as I was able to travel. The Major secured and paid for a state-room in a sleeper the day before we left, so that I could have plenty of room and be comfortable; but when we arrived at the station a mistake

had been made and our car had not been put
on. The conductor had reserved a section for
us—it was the best he could do, he said. But
the Major said we were not in a hurry, and
would wait for the car to be put on. The
conductor responded, with pleasant irony:

"It may be that *you* are not in a hurry, just
as you say, but we *are*. Come, get aboard,
gentlemen, get aboard—don't keep us waiting."

But the Major would not get aboard himself nor allow me to do it. He wanted his
car, and said he must have it. This made the
hurried and perspiring conductor impatient,
and he said:

"It's the best we can *do*—we can't do im-
possibilities. You will take the section or go
without. A mistake has been made and can't
be rectified at this late hour. It's a thing that
happens now and then, and there is nothing
for it but to put up with it and make the best
of it. Other people do."

"Ah, that is just it, you see. If they had
stuck to their rights and enforced them you
wouldn't be trying to trample mine under-
foot in this bland way now. I haven't any
disposition to give you unnecessary trouble,
but it is my duty to protect the next man from

this kind of imposition. So I must have
my car. Otherwise I will wait in Chicago
and sue the company for violating its con-
tract."

"Sue the company?—for a thing like that!"

"Certainly."

"Do you really mean that?"

"Indeed, I do."

The conductor looked the Major over won-
deringly, and then said:

"It beats me—it's bran-new—I've never
struck the mate to it before. But I swear I
think you'd do it. Look here, I'll send for the
station-master."

When the station-master came he was a
good deal annoyed—at the Major, not at the
person who had made the mistake. He was
rather brusque, and took the same position
which the conductor had taken in the beginning; but he failed to move the soft-spoken
artilleryman, who still insisted that he must
have his car. However, it was plain that there
was only one strong side in this case, and that
that side was the Major's. The station-master banished his annoyed manner, and became
pleasant and even half-apologetic. This made
a good opening for a compromise, and the
Major made a concession. He said he would

give up the engaged state-room, but he must
have *a* state-room.   After a deal of ransacking,
one was found whose owner was persuadable;
he exchanged it for our section, and we got
away at last.   The conductor called on us in
the evening, and was kind and courteous and
obliging, and we had a long talk and got to be
good friends.   He said he wished the public
would make trouble oftener—it would have
a good effect.   He said that the railroads could
not be expected to do their whole duty by
the traveller unless the traveller would take
some interest in the matter himself.

I hoped that we were done reforming for
the trip now, but it was not so.   In the hotel-
car, in the morning, the Major called for broiled
chicken.   The waiter said:

"It's not in the bill of fare, sir; we do not
serve anything but what is in the bill."

"That gentleman yonder is eating a broiled
chicken."

"Yes, but that is different.   He is one of
the superintendents of the road."

"Then all the more must I have broiled
chicken.   I do not like these discriminations.
Please hurry—bring me a broiled chicken."

The waiter brought the steward, who explained in a low and polite voice that the

thing was impossible—it was against the rule, and the rule was rigid.

"Very well, then, you must either apply it impartially or break it impartially. You must take that gentleman's chicken away from him or bring me one."

The steward was puzzled, and did not quite know what to do. He began an incoherent argument, but the conductor came along just then, and asked what the difficulty was. The steward explained that here was a gentleman who was insisting on having a chicken when it was dead against the rule and not in the bill. The conductor said:

"Stick by your rules—you haven't any option. Wait a moment—is this the gentleman?" Then he laughed and said: "Never mind your rules—it's my advice, and sound; give him anything he wants—don't get him started on his rights. Give him whatever he asks for; and if you haven't got it, stop the train and get it."

The Major ate the chicken, but said he did it from a sense of duty and to establish a principle, for he did not like chicken.

I missed the Fair it is true, but I picked up some diplomatic tricks which I and the reader may find handy and useful as we go along.

10

PRIVATE HISTORY OF THE "JUMPING
FROG" STORY

PRIVATE HISTORY OF THE "JUMPING FROG" STORY

FIVE or six years ago a lady from Finland asked me to tell her a story in our negro dialect, so that she could get an idea of what that variety of speech was like. I told her one of Hopkinson Smith's negro stories, and gave her a copy of *Harper's Monthly* containing it. She translated it for a Swedish newspaper, but by an oversight named me as the author of it instead of Smith. I was very sorry for that, because I got a good lashing in the Swedish press, which would have fallen to his share but for that mistake; for it was shown that Boccaccio had told that very story, in his curt and meagre fashion, five hundred years before Smith took hold of it and made a good and tellable thing out of it.

I have always been sorry for Smith. But my own turn has come now. A few weeks ago Professor Van Dyke, of Princeton, asked this question:

"Do you know how old your Jumping Frog story is?"

And I answered:

"Yes — forty-five years. The thing happened in Calaveras County in the spring of 1849."

"No; it happened earlier — a couple of thousand years earlier; it is a Greek story."

I was astonished—and hurt. I said:

" I am willing to be a literary thief if it has been so ordained; I am even willing to be caught robbing the ancient dead alongside of Hopkinson Smith, for he is my friend and a good fellow, and I think would be as honest as any one if he could do it without occasioning remark; but I am not willing to antedate his crimes by fifteen hundred years. I must ask you to knock off part of that."

But the professor was not chaffing; he was in earnest, and could not abate a century. He named the Greek author, and offered to get the book and send it to me and the college text-book containing the English translation also. I thought I would like the translation best, because Greek makes me tired. January 30th he sent me the English version, and I will presently insert it in this article. It is my Jumping Frog tale in every essential. It is not strung out as I have strung it out, but it is all there.

To me this is very curious and interesting. Curious for several reasons. For instance:

I heard the story told by a man who was not telling it to his hearers as a thing new to them, but as a thing which *they had witnessed and would remember*. He was a dull person, and ignorant; he had no gift as a story-teller, and no invention; in his mouth this episode was merely history — history and statistics; and the gravest sort of history, too; he was entirely serious, for he was dealing with what to him were austere facts, and they interested him solely because they *were* facts; he was drawing on his memory, not his mind; he saw no humor in his tale, neither did his listeners; neither he nor they ever smiled or laughed; in my time I have not attended a more solemn conference. To him and to his fellow gold-miners there were just two things in the story that were worth considering. One was the smartness of its hero, Jim Smiley, in taking the stranger in with a loaded frog; and the other was Smiley's deep knowledge of a frog's nature—for he knew (as the narrator asserted and the listeners conceded) that a frog *likes shot* and is always ready to eat it. Those men discussed those two points, and those only. They were hearty in their admiration of them, and none of the party was aware that a first-rate story had been told in a first-rate way, and that it was brimful of a quality whose presence they never suspected—humor.

Now, then, the interesting question is, *did* the frog episode happen in Angel's Camp in the spring of '49, as told in my hearing that day in the fall of 1865? I am perfectly sure that it did. I am also sure that its duplicate happened in Bœotia a couple of thousand years ago. I think it must be a case of history actually repeating itself, and not a case of a good story floating down the ages and surviving because too good to be allowed to perish.

I would now like to have the reader examine the Greek story and the story told by the dull and solemn Californian, and observe how exactly alike they are in essentials.

[*Translation.*]

THE ATHENIAN AND THE FROG.*

An Athenian once fell in with a Bœotian who was sitting by the road-side looking at a frog. Seeing the other approach, the Bœotian said his was a remarka-

* Sidgwick, *Greek Prose Composition*, page 116.

ble frog, and asked if he would agree to start a contest of frogs, on condition that he whose frog jumped farthest should receive a large sum of money. The Athenian replied that he would if the other would fetch him a frog, for the lake was near. To this he agreed, and when he was gone the Athenian took the frog, and, opening its mouth, poured some stones into its stomach, so that it did not indeed seem larger than before, but could not jump. The Bœotian soon returned with the other frog, and the contest began. The second frog first was pinched, and jumped moderately; then they pinched the Bœotian frog. And he gathered himself for a leap, and used the utmost effort, but he could not move his body the least. So the Athenian departed with the money. When he was gone the Bœotian, wondering what was the matter with the frog, lifted him up and examined him. And being turned upside down, he opened his mouth and vomited out the stones.

And here is the way it happened in California:

FROM "THE CELEBRATED JUMPING FROG OF CALAVERAS COUNTY."

Well, thish-yer Smiley had rat-tarriers, and chicken cocks, and tom-cats, and all them kind of things, till you couldn't rest, and you couldn't fetch nothing for him to bet on but he'd match you. He ketched a frog one day, and took him home, and said he cal'lated to educate him; and so he never done nothing for three months but set in his back yard and learn that frog to jump. And you bet you he *did* learn him, too. He'd give him a little punch behind, and the next minute you'd see that frog whirling in the air like a doughnut—see him turn one summerset, or maybe a couple if he got a good start, and come down flat-footed and all right, like a cat. He got him up so in the matter of ketching flies, and kep' him in practice so constant, that he'd nail a fly every time as fur as he could see him. Smiley said all a frog wanted was education, and he could do 'most anything — and I believe him. Why, I've seen him set Dan'l Webster down here on this floor—Dan'l Webster was the name of the frog — and sing out "Flies, Dan'l, flies!" and quicker'n you could wink he'd spring straight up and snake a fly off'n the counter there, and flop down on the floor ag'in as solid as a gob of mud, and fall to scratching the side of his head with his hind foot as indifferent as if he hadn't no idea he'd been doin' any more'n any frog might do. You never see a frog so modest and straightfor'ard as he was, for all he was so gifted. And when it come to fair and square jumping on a dead level, he could get over more ground at one straddle than any animal of his breed you ever see. Jumping on a dead level was his strong suit, you understand; and when it came to that, Smiley would ante up money on him as long as he had a red. Smiley was monstrous proud of his frog, and well he might be, for fellers that had travelled and been every-wheres all said he laid over any frog that ever *they* see.

Well, Smiley kep' the beast in a little lattice box, and he used to fetch him down-town sometimes and lay for a bet. One day a feller—a stranger in the camp, he was—come acrost him with his box, and says:

"What might it be that you've got in the box?"

And Smiley says, sorter indifferent-like, "It might be a parrot, or it might be a canary, maybe, but it ain't—it's only just a frog."

And the feller took it, and looked at it careful, and turned it round this way and that, and says, "H'm—so 'tis. Well, what's *he* good for?"

"Well," Smiley says, easy and careless, "he's good enough for *one* thing, I should judge—he can outjump any frog in Calaveras County."

The feller took the box again and took another long, particular look, and give it back to Smiley and says, very deliberate, "Well," he says, "I don't see no p'ints about that frog that's any better'n any other frog."

"Maybe you don't," Smiley says. "Maybe you understand frogs and maybe you don't understand 'em; maybe you've had experience, and maybe you ain't only a amature, as it were. Anyways, I've got *my* opinion, and I'll resk forty dollars that he can outjump any frog in Calaveras County."

And the feller studies a minute, and then says, kinder sad like, "Well, I'm only a stranger here, and I ain't got no frog, but if I had a frog I'd bet you."

And then Smiley says: "That's all right—that's all right—if you'll hold my box a minute, I'll go and get you a frog." And so the feller took the box and put up his forty dollars along with Smiley's and set down to wait.

So he set there a good while thinking and thinking to hisself, and then he got the frog out and prized his

mouth open and took a teaspoon and filled him full
of quail shot—filled him pretty near up to his chin—
and set him on the floor. Smiley he went to the
swamp and slopped around in the mud for a long
time, and finally he ketched a frog and fetched him
in and give him to this feller, and says:

" Now, if you're ready, set him alongside of Dan'l,
with his fore-paws just even with Dan'l's, and I'll give
the word." Then he says, " One—two—three—*git!*"
and him and the feller touched up the frogs from behind, and the new frog hopped off lively; but Dan'l
give a heave, and hysted up his shoulders—so—like a
Frenchman, but it warn't no use—he couldn't budge;
he was planted as solid as a church, and he couldn't
no more stir than if he was anchored out. Smiley
was a good deal surprised, and he was disgusted, too,
but he didn't have no idea what the matter was, of
course.

The feller took the money and started away; and
when he was going out at the door he sorter jerked
his thumb over his shoulder—so—at Dan'l, and says
again, very deliberate: " Well," he says, " *I* don't see
no p'ints about that frog that's any better'n any other
frog."

Smiley he stood scratching his head and looking
down at Dan'l a long time, and at last he says, " I do
wonder what in the nation that frog throw'd off for—
I wonder if there ain't something the matter with
him — he 'pears to look mighty baggy, somehow."
And he ketched Dan'l by the nap of the neck, and
hefted him, and says, " Why, blame my cats if he don't
weigh five pound!" and turned him upside down, and
he belched out a double handful of shot. And then

he see how it was, and he was the maddest man—he set the frog down and took out after that feller, but he never ketched him.

The resemblances are deliciously exact. There you have the wily Bœotian and the wily Jim Smiley waiting—two thousand years apart—and waiting, each equipped with his frog and "laying" for the stranger. A contest is proposed—for money. The Athenian would take a chance "if the other would fetch him a frog"; the Yankee says: "I'm only a stranger here, and I ain't got no frog; but if I had a frog I'd bet you." The wily Bœotian and the wily Californian, with that vast gulf of two thousand years between, retire eagerly and go frogging in the marsh; the Athenian and the Yankee remain behind and work a base advantage, the one with pebbles, the other with shot. Presently the contest began. In the one case "they pinched the Bœotian frog"; in the other, "him and the feller touched up the frogs from behind." The Bœotian frog "gathered himself for a leap" (you can just *see* him!), but "could not move his body in the least"; the Californian frog "give a heave, but it warn't no use—he couldn't budge." In both the ancient and the modern cases the strangers departed with the money. The Bœo-

tian and the Californian wonder what is the
matter with their frogs; they lift them and
examine; they turn them upside down and
out spills the informing ballast.

Yes, the resemblances are curiously exact.
I used to tell the story of the Jumping Frog
in San Francisco, and presently Artemus Ward
came along and wanted it to help fill out a little book which he was about to publish; so
I wrote it out and sent it to his publisher,
Carleton; but Carleton thought the book had
enough matter in it, so he gave the story to
Henry Clapp as a present, and Clapp put it in
his *Saturday Press*, and it killed that paper
with a suddenness that was beyond praise. At
least the paper died with that issue, and none
but envious people have ever tried to rob me
of the honor and credit of killing it. The
"Jumping Frog" was the first piece of writing of mine that spread itself through the
newspapers and brought me into public notice.
Consequently, the *Saturday Press* was a cocoon
and I the worm in it; also, I was the gay-col-
ored literary moth which its death set free.
This simile has been used before.

Early in '66 the "Jumping Frog" was issued in book form, with other sketches of mine.
A year or two later Madame Blanc translated

it into French and published it in the *Revue des Deux Mondes*, but the result was not what should have been expected, for the *Revue* struggled along and pulled through, and is alive yet. I think the fault must have been in the translation. I ought to have translated it myself. I think so because I examined into the matter and finally retranslated the sketch from the French back into English, to see what the trouble was; that is, to see just what sort of a focus the French people got upon it. Then the mystery was explained. In French the story is too confused, and chaotic, and unreposeful, and ungrammatical, and insane; consequently it could only cause grief and sickness—it could not kill. A glance at my re-translation will show the reader that this must be true.

[*My Retranslation.*]

THE FROG JUMPING OF THE COUNTY OF CALAVERAS.

Eh bien! this Smiley nourished some terriers à rats, and some cocks of combat, and some cats, and all sort of things; and with his rage of betting one no had more of repose. He trapped one day a frog and him imported with him (et l'emporta chez lui) saying that he pretended to make his education. You me believe if you will, but during three months he not has nothing done but to him apprehend to jump (apprendre a sauter) in a court retired of her mansion (de sa maison).

And I you respond that he have succeeded. He him gives a small blow by behind, and the instant after you shall see the frog turn in the air like a grease-biscuit, make one summersault, sometimes two, when she was well started, and re-fall upon his feet like a cat. He him had accomplished in the art of to gobble the flies (gober des mouches), and him there exercised continually—so well that a fly at the most far that she appeared was a fly lost. Smiley had custom to say that all which lacked to a frog it was the education, but with the education she could do nearly all —and I him believe. Tenez, I him have seen pose Daniel Webster there upon this plank—Daniel Webster was the name of the frog—and to him sing, "Some flies, Daniel, some flies!"—in a flash of the eye Daniel had bounded and seized a fly here upon the counter, then jumped anew at the earth, where he rested truly to himself scratch the head with his behind-foot, as if he no had not the least idea of his superiority. Never you not have seen frog as modest, as natural, sweet as she was. And when he himself agitated to jump purely and simply upon plain earth, she does more ground in one jump than any beast of his species than you can know.

To jump plain—this was his strong. When he himself agitated for that Smiley multiplied the bets upon her as long as there to him remained a red. It must to know, Smiley was monstrously proud of his frog, and he of it was right, for some men who were travelled, who had all seen, said that they to him would be injurious to him compare to another frog. Smiley guarded Daniel in a little box latticed which he carried bytimes to the village for some bet.

One day an individual stranger at the camp him arrested with his box and him said :

"What is this that you have then shut up there within ?"

Smiley said, with an air indifferent :

"That could be a paroquet, or a syringe (*ou un serin*), but this no is nothing of such, it not is but a frog."

The individual it took, it regarded with care, it turned from one side and from the other, then he said :

"*Tiens!* in effect!—At what is she good ?"

"My God!" respond Smiley, always with an air disengaged, "she is good for one thing, to my notice (*à mon avis*), she can batter in jumping (*elle peut batter en sautant*) all frogs of the county of Calaveras."

The individual re-took the box, it examined of new longly, and it rendered to Smiley in saying with an air deliberate :

"*Eh bien!* I no saw not that that frog had nothing of better than each frog." (*Je ne vois pas que cette grenouille ait rien de mieux qu'aucune grenouille*). [If that isn't grammar gone to seed, then I count myself no judge.—M. T.]

"Possible that you not it saw not," said Smiley, "possible that you—you comprehend frogs; possible that you not you there comprehend nothing; possible that you had of the experience, and possible that you not be but an amateur. Of all manner (*De toute manière*) I bet forty dollars that she batter in jumping no matter which frog of the county of Calaveras."

The individual reflected a second, and said like sad :

"I not am but a stranger here, I no have not a frog; but if I of it had one, I would embrace the bet."

11

"Strong, well!" respond Smiley; "nothing of more facility. If you will hold my box a minute, I go you to search a frog (*j'irai vous chercher*)."

Behold, then, the individual, who guards the box, who puts his forty dollars upon those of Smiley, and who attends (*et qui attend*). He attended enough longtimes, reflecting all solely. And figure you that he takes Daniel, him opens the mouth by force and with a teaspoon him fills with shot of the hunt, even him fills just to the chin, then he him puts by the earth. Smiley during these times was at slopping in a swamp. Finally he trapped (*attrape*) a frog, him carried to that individual, and said:

"Now if you be ready, put him all against Daniel, with their before-feet upon the same line, and I give the signal"—then he added: "One, two, three—advance!"

Him and the individual touched their frogs by behind, and the frog new put to jump smartly, but Daniel himself lifted ponderously, exalted the shoulders thus, like a Frenchman—to what good? he could not budge, he is planted solid like a church, he not advance no more than if one him had put at the anchor.

Smiley was surprised and disgusted, but he not himself doubted not of the turn being intended (*mais il ne se doutait pas du tour bien entendu*). The individual empocketed the silver, himself with it went, and of it himself in going is that he no gives not a jerk of thumb over the shoulder—like that—at the poor Daniel, in saying with his air deliberate—(*L'individu empoche l'argent s'en va et en s'en allant est ce qu'il ne donne pas un coup de pouce par-dessus l'épaule, comme ça, au pauvre Daniel, en disant de son air délibéré.*)

"Eh bien! *I no see not that that frog has nothing of better than another.*"

Smiley himself scratched longtimes the head, the eyes fixed upon Daniel, until that which at last he said:

"I me demand how the devil it makes itself that this beast has refused. Is it that she had something? One would believe that she is stuffed."

He grasped Daniel by the skin of the neck, him lifted and said:

"The wolf me bite if he no weigh not five pounds."

He him reversed and the unhappy belched two handfuls of shot (*et le malheureux*, etc.).—When Smiley recognized how it was, he was like mad. He deposited his frog by the earth and ran after that individual, but he not him caught never.

It may be that there are people who can translate better than I can, but I am not acquainted with them.

So ends the private and public history of the Jumping Frog of Calaveras County, an incident which has this unique feature about it —that it is both old and new, a "chestnut" and not a "chestnut"; for it was original when it happened two thousand years ago, and was again original when it happened in California in our own time.

MENTAL TELEGRAPHY AGAIN

MENTAL TELEGRAPHY AGAIN

I HAVE three or four curious incidents to tell about. They seem to come under the head of what I named " Mental Telegraphy " in a paper written seventeen years ago, and published long afterwards.*

Several years ago I made a campaign on the platform with Mr. George W. Cable.   In Montreal we were honored with a reception.   It began at two in the afternoon in a long drawing-room in the Windsor Hotel.   Mr. Cable and I stood at one end of this room, and the ladies and gentlemen entered it at the other end, crossed it at that end, then came up the long left-hand side, shook hands with us, said a word or two, and passed on, in the usual way.   My sight is of the telescopic sort, and I presently recognized a familiar face among the throng of strangers drifting in at the dis-

* The paper entitled " Mental Telegraphy," which originally appeared in HARPER'S MAGAZINE for December 1893, is included in the volume entitled *The American Claimant, and Other Stories and Sketches.*

tant door, and I said to myself, with surprise and high gratification, " That is Mrs. R.; I had forgotten that she was a Canadian." She had been a great friend of mine in Carson City, Nevada, in the early days. I had not seen her or heard of her for twenty years; I had not been thinking about her; there was nothing to suggest her to me, nothing to bring her to my mind; in fact, to me she had long ago ceased to exist, and had disappeared from my consciousness. But I knew her instantly; and I saw her so clearly that I was able to note some of the particulars of her dress, and did note them, and they remained in my mind. I was impatient for her to come. In the midst of the hand-shakings I snatched glimpses of her and noted her progress with the slow-moving file across the end of the room; then I saw her start up the side, and this gave me a full front view of her face. I saw her last when she was within twenty-five feet of me. For an hour I kept thinking she must still be in the room somewhere and would come at last, but I was disappointed.

When I arrived in the lecture-hall that evening some one said: " Come into the waiting-room; there's a friend of yours there who wants to see you. You'll not be introduced—

you are to do the recognizing without help if you can."

I said to myself: "It is Mrs. R.; I sha'n't have any trouble."

There were perhaps ten ladies present, all seated. In the midst of them was Mrs. R., as I had expected. She was dressed exactly as she was when I had seen her in the afternoon. I went forward and shook hands with her and called her by name, and said:

"I knew you the moment you appeared at the reception this afternoon."

She looked surprised, and said: "But I was not at the reception. I have just arrived from Quebec, and have not been in town an hour."

It was my turn to be surprised now. I said: "I can't help it. I give you my word of honor that it is as I say. I saw you at the reception, and you were dressed precisely as you are now. When they told me a moment ago that I should find a friend in this room, your image rose before me, dress and all, just as I had seen you at the reception."

Those are the facts. She was not at the reception at all, or anywhere near it; but I saw her there nevertheless, and most clearly and unmistakably. To that I could make oath.

How is one to explain this? I was not thinking of her at the time; had not thought of her for years. But she had been thinking of me, no doubt; did her thoughts flit through leagues of air to me, and bring with it that clear and pleasant vision of herself? I think so. That was and remains my sole experience in the matter of apparitions—I mean apparitions that come when one is (ostensibly) awake. I could have been asleep for a moment; the apparition could have been the creature of a dream. Still, that is nothing to the point; the feature of interest is the happening of the thing just at that time, instead of at an earlier or later time, which is argument that its origin lay in thought-transference.

My next incident will be set aside by most persons as being merely a " coincidence," I suppose. Years ago I used to think sometimes of making a lecturing trip through the antipodes and the borders of the Orient, but always gave up the idea, partly because of the great length of the journey and partly because my wife could not well manage to go with me. Towards the end of last January that idea, after an interval of years, came suddenly into my head again—forcefully, too, and without any apparent reason. Whence came it? What suggested it? I will touch upon that presently.

I was at that time where I am now — in Paris. I wrote at once to Henry M. Stanley (London), and asked him some questions about his Australian lecture tour, and inquired who had conducted him and what were the terms. After a day or two his answer came. It began:

"The lecture agent for Australia and New Zealand is *par excellence* Mr. R. S. Smythe, of Melbourne."

He added his itinerary, terms, sea expenses, and some other matters, and advised me to write Mr. Smythe, which I did—February 3d. I began my letter by saying in substance that while he did not know me personally we had a mutual friend in Stanley, and that would answer for an introduction. Then I proposed my trip, and asked if he would give me the same terms which he had given Stanley.

I mailed my letter to Mr. Smythe February 6th, and three days later I got a letter from the selfsame Smythe, dated Melbourne, December 17th. I would as soon have expected to get a letter from the late George Washington. The letter began somewhat as mine to him had begun—with a self-introduction:

"DEAR MR. CLEMENS,—It is so long since Archibald Forbes and I spent that pleasant afternoon in your comfortable house at Hartford that you have probably quite forgotten the occasion."

In the course of his letter this occurs:

"I am willing to give you" [here he named the terms which he had given Stanley] "for an antipodean tour to last, say, three months."

Here was the single essential detail of my letter answered three days after I had mailed my inquiry. I might have saved myself the trouble and the postage — and a few years ago I would have done that very thing, for I would have argued that my sudden and strong impulse to write and ask some questions of a stranger on the under side of the globe meant that the impulse came from that stranger, and that he would answer my questions of his own motion if I would let him alone.

Mr. Smythe's letter probably passed under my nose on its way to lose three weeks travelling to America and back, and gave me a whiff of its contents as it went along. Letters often act like that. Instead of the *thought* coming to you in an instant from Australia, the (apparently) unsentient letter imparts it to you as it glides invisibly past your elbow in the mail-bag.

Next incident. In the following month—March—I was in America. I spent a Sunday at Irvington-on-the-Hudson with Mr. John Brisben Walker, of the *Cosmopolitan* magazine. We came into New York next morning, and went to the Century Club for luncheon. He said some praiseful things about the character of the club and the orderly serenity and pleasantness of its quarters, and asked if I had never tried to acquire membership in it. I said I had not, and that New York clubs were a continuous expense to the country members without being of frequent use or benefit to them.

"And now I've got an idea!" said I. "There's the Lotos—the first New York club I was ever a member of — my very earliest love in that line. I have been a member of it for considerably more than twenty years, yet have seldom had a chance to look in and see the boys. They turn gray and grow old while I am not watching. And *my dues go on.* I am going to Hartford this afternoon for a day or two, but as soon as I get back I will go to John Elderkin very privately and say: 'Remember the veteran and confer distinction upon him, for the sake of old times. Make me an honorary member and abolish the tax. If you haven't any such thing as honorary membership, all the better—create it for my honor and glory.' That would be a great thing; I will go to John Elderkin as soon as I get back from Hartford."

I took the last express that afternoon, first telegraphing Mr. F. G. Whitmore to come and see me next day.   When he came he asked:

"Did you get a letter from Mr. John Elderkin, secretary of the Lotos Club, before you left New York?"

"No."

"Then it just missed you.   If I had known you were coming I would have kept it.   It is beautiful, and will make you proud.   The Board of Directors, by unanimous vote, have made you a life member, and *squelched those dues;* and you are to be on hand and receive your distinction on the night of the 30th, which is the twenty-fifth anniversary of the founding of the club, and it will not surprise me if they have some great times there."

What put the honorary membership in my head that day in the Century Club? for I had never thought of it before.   I don't know what brought the thought to me at *that* particular time instead of earlier, but I am well satisfied that it originated with the Board of Directors, and had been on its way to my brain through the air ever since the moment that saw their vote recorded.

Another incident. I was in Hartford two or three days as a guest of the Rev. Joseph H. Twichell. I have held the rank of Honorary Uncle to his children for a quarter of a century, and I went out with him in the trolley-car to visit one of my nieces, who is at Miss Porter's famous school in Farmington. The distance is eight or nine miles. On the way, talking, I illustrated something with an anecdote. This is the anecdote:

Two years and a half ago I and the family arrived at Milan on our way to Rome, and stopped at the Continental. After dinner I went below and took a seat in the stone-paved court, where the customary lemon-trees stand in the customary tubs, and said to myself, "Now *this* is comfort, comfort and repose, and nobody to disturb it; I do not know anybody in Milan."

Then a young gentleman stepped up and shook hands, which damaged my theory. He said, in substance:

"You won't remember me, Mr. Clemens, but I remember you very well. I was a cadet at West Point when you and Rev. Joseph H. Twichell came there some years ago and talked

to us on a Hundredth Night. I am a lieutenant in the regular army now, and my name
is H. I am in Europe, all alone, for a modest
little tour; my regiment is in Arizona."

We became friendly and sociable, and in the
course of the talk he told me of an adventure
which had befallen him—about to this effect:

"I was at Bellagio, stopping at the big
hotel there, and ten days ago I lost my letter
of credit. I did not know what in the world
to do. I was a stranger; I knew no one in
Europe; I hadn't a penny in my pocket; I
couldn't even send a telegram to London to
get my lost letter replaced; my hotel bill was
a week old, and the presentation of it imminent—so imminent that it could happen at
any moment now. I was so frightened that
my wits seemed to leave me. I tramped and
tramped, back and forth, like a crazy person.
If anybody approached me I hurried away,
for no matter what a person looked like, I took
him for the head waiter with the bill.

"I was at last in such a desperate state that
I was ready to do any wild thing that promised
even the shadow of help, and so this is the
insane thing that I did. I saw a family lunch-
ing at a small table on the veranda, and recognized their nationality—Americans—father,

mother, and several young daughters—young, tastefully dressed, and pretty—the rule with our people. I went straight there in my civilian costume, named my name, said I was a lieutenant in the army, and told my story and asked for help.

"What do you suppose the gentleman did? But you would not guess in twenty years. He took out a handful of gold coin and told me to help myself—freely. That is what he did."

The next morning the lieutenant told me his new letter of credit had arrived in the night, so we strolled to Cook's to draw money to pay back the benefactor with. We got it, and then went strolling through the great arcade. Presently he said, "Yonder they are; come and be introduced." I was introduced to the parents and the young ladies; then we separated, and I never saw him or them any m—

"Here we are at Farmington," said Twichell, interrupting.

We left the trolley-car and tramped through the mud a hundred yards or so to the school, talking about the time we and Warner walked out there years ago, and the pleasant time we had.

We had a visit with my niece in the parlor,

12

then started for the trolley again. Outside
the house we encountered a double rank of
twenty or thirty of Miss Porter's young ladies
arriving from a walk, and we stood aside, ostensibly to let them have room to file past,
but really to look at them. Presently one of
them stepped out of the rank and said:

"You don't know me, Mr. Twichell, but I
know your daughter, and that gives me the
privilege of shaking hands with you."

Then she put out her hand to me, and said:

"And I wish to shake hands with you too,
Mr. Clemens. You don't remember me, but
you were introduced to me in the arcade in
Milan two years and a half ago by Lieutenant H."

What had put that story into my head after
all that stretch of time? Was it just the
proximity of that young girl, or was it merely
an odd accident?

WHAT PAUL BOURGET THINKS OF US

WHAT PAUL BOURGET THINKS OF US

HE reports the American joke correctly. In Boston they ask, How much does he know? in New York, How much is he worth? in Philadelphia, Who were his parents? And when an alien observer turns his telescope upon us —advertisedly in our own special interest—a natural apprehension moves us to ask, What is the diameter of his reflector?

I take a great interest in M. Bourget's chapters, for I know by the newspapers that there are several Americans who are expecting to get a whole education out of them; several who foresaw, and also foretold, that our long night was over, and a light almost divine about to break upon the land.

"His utterances concerning us are bound to be weighty and well timed."

"He gives us an object-lesson which should be thoughtfully and profitably studied."

These well-considered and important verdicts were of a nature to restore public confidence, which had been disquieted by questionings as to whether so young a teacher would be qualified to take so large a class as 70,000,-000, distributed over so extensive a schoolhouse as America, and pull it through without assistance.

I was even disquieted myself, although I am of a cold, calm temperament, and not easily disturbed. I feared for my country. And I was not wholly tranquillized by the verdicts rendered as above. It seemed to me that there was still room for doubt. In fact, in looking the ground over I became more disturbed than I was before. Many worrying questions came up in my mind. Two were prominent. Where had the teacher gotten his equipment? What was his method?

He had gotten his equipment in France.

Then as to his method: I saw by his own intimations that he was an Observer, and had a System—that used by naturalists and other scientists. The naturalist collects many bugs and reptiles and butterflies and studies their ways a long time patiently. By this means he is presently able to group these creatures into families and subdivisions of families by nice shadings of differences observable in their char-

acters. Then he labels all those shaded bugs
and things with nicely descriptive group names,
and is now happy, for his great work is com-
pleted, and as a result he intimately knows
every bug and shade of a bug there, inside and
out. It may be true, but a person who was
not a naturalist would feel safer about it if he
had the opinion of the bug. I think it is a
pleasant System, but subject to error.

The Observer of Peoples has to be a Classi-
fier, a Grouper, a Deducer, a Generalizer, a
Psychologizer; and, first and last, a Thinker.
He has to be all these, and when he is at
home, observing his own folk, he is often able
to prove competency. But history has shown
that when he is abroad observing unfamiliar
peoples the chances are heavily against him.
He is then a naturalist observing a bug, with
no more than a naturalist's chance of being
able to tell the bug anything new about itself,
and no more than a naturalist's chance of being able to teach it any new ways which it
will prefer to its own.

To return to that first question. M. Bourget,
as teacher, would simply be France teaching
America. It seemed to me that the outlook
was dark—almost Egyptian, in fact. What
would the new teacher, representing France,

teach us? Railroading? No. France knows nothing valuable about railroading. Steam-shipping? No. France has no superiorities over us in that matter. Steamboating? No. French steamboating is still of Fulton's date—1809. Postal service? No. France is a back number there. Telegraphy? No, we taught her that ourselves. Journalism? No. Mag-azining? No, that is our own specialty. Gov-ernment? No; Liberty, Equality, Fraternity, Nobility, Democracy, Adultery—the system is too variegated for our climate. Religion? No, not variegated enough for our climate. Morals? No, we cannot rob the poor to en-rich ourselves. Novel-writing? No. M. Bourget and the others know only one plan, and when that is expurgated there is nothing left of the book.

I wish I could think what he is going to teach us. Can it be Deportment? But he experimented in that at Newport and failed to give satisfaction, except to a few. Those few are pleased. They are enjoying their joy as well as they can. They confess their hap-piness to the interviewer. They feel pretty striped, but they remember with reverent rec-ognition that they had sugar between the cuts. True, sugar with sand in it, but sugar. And true, they had some trouble to tell which was sugar and which was sand, because the sugar itself looked just like the sand, and also had a gravelly taste; still, they knew that the sugar was there, and would have been very good sugar indeed if it had been screened. Yes, they are pleased; not noisily so, but pleased; invaded, or streaked, as one may say, with little recurrent shivers of joy—subdued joy, so to speak, not the overdone kind. And they commune together, these, and massage each other with comforting sayings, in a sweet spirit of resignation and thankfulness, mixing these elements in the same proportions as the sugar and the sand, as a memorial, and saying, the one to the other and to the interviewer: " It was severe—yes, it was bitterly severe; but oh, how true it was; and it will do us so much good!"

If it isn't Deportment, what is left? It was at this point that I seemed to get on the right track at last. M. Bourget would teach us to know ourselves; that was it: he would reveal us to ourselves. That would be an education. He would explain us to ourselves. Then we should understand ourselves; and after that be able to go on more intelligently.

It seemed a doubtful scheme. He could

explain *us* to *him*self — that would be easy.
That would be the same as the naturalist explaining the bug to himself. But to explain
the bug to the bug—that is quite a different
matter. The bug may not know himself perfectly, but he knows himself better than the
naturalist can know him, at any rate.

A foreigner can photograph the exteriors of
a nation, but I think that that is as far as he
can get. I think that no foreigner can report
its interior — its soul, its life, its speech, its
thought. I think that a knowledge of these
things is acquirable in only one way; not two
or four or six—*absorption;* years and years of
unconscious absorption; years and years of
intercourse with the life concerned; of living
it, indeed; sharing personally in its shames
and prides, its joys and griefs, its loves and
hates, its prosperities and reverses, its shows
and shabbinesses, its deep patriotisms, its whirlwinds of political passion, its adorations—of
flag, and heroic dead, and the glory of the national name. Observation? Of what real
value is it? One learns peoples through the
heart, not the eyes or the intellect.

There is only one expert who is qualified to
examine the souls and the life of a people and
make a valuable report—the native novelist.

This expert is so rare that the most populous country can never have fifteen conspicuously and confessedly competent ones in stock at one time. This native specialist is not qualified to begin work until he has been absorbing during twenty-five years. How much of his competency is derived from conscious " observation "? The amount is so slight that it counts for next to nothing in the equipment. Almost the whole capital of the novelist is the slow accumulation of *un*conscious observation —absorption. The native expert's intentional observation of manners, speech, character, and ways of life can have value, for the native knows what they mean without having to ciper out the meaning. But I should be astonished to see a foreigner get at the right meanings, catch the elusive shades of these subtle things. Even the native novelist becomes a foreigner, with a foreigner's limitations, when he steps from the State whose life is familiar to him into a State whose life he has not lived. Bret Harte got his California and his Californians by unconscious absorption, and put both of them into his tales alive. But when he came from the Pacific to the Atlantic and tried to do Newport life from study —conscious observation—his failure was abso-

lutely monumental. Newport is a disastrous
place for the unacclimated observer, evidently.

To return to novel-building. Does the native novelist try to generalize the nation? No,
he lays plainly before you the ways and speech
and life of a few people grouped in a certain
place—his own place—and that is one book.
In time he and his brethren will report to you
the life and the people of the whole nation—
the life of a group in a New England village;
in a New York village; in a Texan village;
in an Oregon village; in villages in fifty States
and Territories; then the farm-life in fifty States
and Territories; a hundred patches of life and
groups of people in a dozen widely separated
cities. And the Indians will be attended to;
and the cowboys; and the gold and silver
miners; and the negroes; and the Idiots and
Congressmen; and the Irish, the Germans, the
Italians, the Swedes, the French, the China-
men, the Greasers; and the Catholics, the
Methodists, the Presbyterians, the Congrega-
tionalists, the Baptists, the Spiritualists, the
Mormons, the Shakers, the Quakers, the Jews,
the Campbellites, the infidels, the Christian
Scientists, the Mind-Curists, the Faith-Curists,
the train-robbers, the White Caps, the Moon-
shiners. And when a thousand able novels

have been written, *there* you have the soul of
the people, the life of the people, the speech
of the people ; and not anywhere else can these
be had.   And the shadings of character, manners, feelings, ambitions, will be infinite.

" *The nature of a people* is always of a similar shade
in its vices and its virtues, in its frivolities and in its
labor. *It is this physiognomy which it is necessary to
discover*, and every document is good, from the hall
of a casino to the church, from the foibles of a fashionable woman to the suggestions of a revolutionary
leader.   I am therefore quite sure that this *American
soul*, the principal interest and the great object of my
voyage, appears behind the records of Newport for
those who choose to see it."—*M. Paul Bourget.*

[The italics are mine.]   It is a large con-
tract which he has undertaken.   "Records"
is a pretty poor word there, but I think the
use of it is due to hasty translation.   In the
original the word is *fastes.*   I think M. Bourget meant to suggest that he expected to find
the great "American soul" secreted behind
the *ostentations* of Newport ; and that he was
going to get it out and examine it, and generalize it, and psychologize it, and make it reveal
to him its hidden vast mystery: "the nature
of the people" of the United States of America.   We have been accused of being a natio·

addicted to inventing wild schemes. I trust
that we shall be allowed to retire to second
place now.

There isn't a single human characteristic
that can be safely labelled " American." There
isn't a single human ambition, or religious
trend, or drift of thought, or peculiarity of education, or code of principles, or breed of folly,
or style of conversation, or preference for a
particular subject for discussion, or form of
legs or trunk or head or face or expression or
complexion, or gait, or dress, or manners, or
disposition, or any other human detail, inside
or outside, that can rationally be generalized
as " American."

Whenever you have found what seems to be
an " American " peculiarity, you have only to
cross a frontier or two, or go down or up in
the social scale, and you perceive that it has
disappeared. And you can cross the Atlantic
and find it again. There may be a Newport
religious drift or sporting drift, or conversational style or complexion, or cut of face, but
there are entire empires in America, north,
south, east, and west, where you could not
find your duplicates. It is the same with
everything else which one might propose to
all " American." M. Bourget thinks he has

found the American Coquette. If he had really found her he would also have found, I am sure, that she was not new, that she exists in other lands in the same forms, and with the same frivolous heart and the same ways and impulses. I think this because I have seen our coquette; I have seen her in life; better still, I have seen her in our novels, and seen her twin in foreign novels. I wish M. Bourget had seen ours. He thought he saw her. And so he applied his System to her. She was a Species. So he gathered a number of samples of what seemed to be her, and put them under his glass, and divided them into groups which he calls "types," and labelled them in his usual scientific way with "formulas"—brief sharp descriptive flashes that make a person blink, sometimes, they are so sudden and vivid. As a rule they are pretty far-fetched, but that is not an important matter; they surprise, they compel admiration, and I notice by some of the comments which his efforts have called forth that they deceive the unwary. Here are a few of the coquette variants which he has grouped and labelled:

THE COLLECTOR.

THE EQUILIBREE.

THE PROFESSIONAL BEAUTY.

THE BLUFFER.

THE GIRL-BOY.

If he had stopped with describing these
characters we should have been obliged to believe that they exist; that they exist, and that
he has seen them and spoken with them. But
he did not stop there; he went further and
furnished to us light-throwing samples of their
behavior, and also light - throwing samples of
their speeches. He entered those things in
his note-book without suspicion, he takes them
out and delivers them to the world with a
candor and simplicity which show that he believed them genuine. They throw altogether
too much light. They reveal to the native
the origin of his find. I suppose he knows
how he came to make that novel and capti-
vating discovery, by this time. If he does
not, any American can tell him—any American to whom he will show his anecdotes. It
was "put up" on him, as we say. It was a
jest—to be plain, it was a series of frauds. To
my mind it was a poor sort of jest, witless and
contemptible. The players of it have their
reward, such as it is; they have exhibited the
fact that whatever they may be they are not
ladies. M. Bourget did not discover a type of
coquette; he merely discovered a type of prac-

tical joker. One may say *the* type of practical joker, for these people are exactly alike all over the world. Their equipment is always the same: a vulgar mind, a puerile wit, a cruel disposition as a rule, and always the spirit of treachery.

In his Chapter IV. M. Bourget has two or three columns gravely devoted to the collating and examining and psychologizing of these sorry little frauds. One is not moved to laugh. There is nothing funny in the situation; it is only pathetic. The stranger gave those people his confidence, and they dishonorably treated him in return.

But one must be allowed to suspect that M. Bourget was a little to blame himself. Even a practical joker has some little judgment. He has to exercise some degree of sagacity in selecting his prey if he would save himself from getting into trouble. In my time I have seldom seen such daring things marketed at any price as these conscienceless folk have worked off at par on this confiding observer. It compels the conviction that there was something about him that bred in those speculators a quite unusual sense of safety, and encouraged them to strain their powers in his behalf. They seem to have satisfied themselves that all he

13

wanted was "significant" facts, and that he was not accustomed to examine the source whence they proceeded. It is plain that there was a sort of conspiracy against him almost from the start—a conspiracy to freight him up with all the strange extravagances those people's decayed brains could invent.

The lengths to which they went are next to incredible. They told him things which surely would have excited any one else's suspicion, but they did not excite his. Consider this:

"There is not in all the United States an entirely nude statue."

If an angel should come down and say such a thing about heaven, a reasonably cautious observer would take that angel's number and inquire a little further before he added it to his catch. What does the present observer do? Adds it. Adds it at once. Adds it, and labels it with this innocent comment:

" This small fact is strangely significant."

It does seem to me that this kind of observing is defective.

Here is another curiosity which some liberal person made him a present of. I should think it ought to have disturbed the deep slumber of his suspicion a little, but it didn't. It was a note from a fog-horn for strenuousness, it seems to me, but the doomed voyager did not catch it. If he had but caught it, it would have saved him from several disasters:

" If the American knows that you are travelling to take notes, he is interested in it, and at the same time rejoices in it, as in a tribute."

Again, this is defective observation. It is human to like to be praised; one can even notice it in the French. But it is not human to like to be ridiculed, even when it comes in the form of a "tribute." I think a little psychologizing ought to have come in there. Something like this: A dog does not like to be ridiculed, a redskin does not like to be ridiculed, a negro does not like to be ridiculed, a Chinaman does not like to be ridiculed; let us deduce from these significant facts this formula: the American's grade being higher than these, and the chain of argument stretching unbroken all the way up to him, there is room for suspicion that the person who said the American likes to be ridiculed, and regards it as a tribute, is not a capable observer.

I feel persuaded that in the matter of psychologizing, a professional is too apt to yield

to the fascinations of the loftier regions of that
great art, to the neglect of its lowlier walks.
Every now and then, at half-hour intervals, M.
Bourget collects a hatful of airy inaccuracies
and dissolves them in a panful of assorted ab-
stractions, and runs the charge into a mould
and turns you out a compact principle which
will explain an American girl, or an American woman, or why new people yearn for old
things, or any other impossible riddle which a
person wants answered.

It seems to be conceded that there are a
few human peculiarities that can be generalized
and located here and there in the world and
named by the name of the nation where they
are found. I wonder what they are. Perhaps one of them is temperament. One speaks
of French vivacity and German gravity and
English stubbornness. There is no American
temperament. The nearest that one can come
at it is to say there are two—the composed
Northern and the impetuous Southern; and
both are found in other countries. Morals?
Purity of women may fairly be called universal
with us, but that is the case in some other
countries. We have no monopoly of it; it
cannot be named American. I think that
there is but a single specialty with us, only

one thing that can be called by the wide name
"American." That is the national devotion
to ice-water. All Germans drink beer, but the
British nation drinks beer, too; so neither of
those peoples is *the* beer-drinking nation. I
suppose we do stand alone in having a drink
that nobody likes but ourselves. When we
have been a month in Europe we lose our
craving for it, and we finally tell the hotel
folk that they needn't provide it any more.
Yet we hardly touch our native shore again,
winter or summer, before we are eager for it.
The reasons for this state of things have not
been psychologized yet. I drop the hint and
say no more.

It is my belief that there are some "national" traits and things scattered about the world
that are mere superstitions, frauds that have
lived so long that they have the solid look of
facts. One of them is the dogma that the
French are the only chaste people in the world.
Ever since I arrived in France this last time I
have been accumulating doubts about that;
and before I leave this sunny land again I will
gather in a few random statistics and psychologize the plausibilities out of it. If people
are to come over to America and find fault
with our girls and our women, and psycholo-

gize every little thing they do, and try to
teach them how to behave, and how to culti-
vate themselves up to where one cannot tell
them from the French model, I intend to find
out whether those missionaries are qualified
or not. A nation ought always to examine
into this detail before engaging the teacher
for good. This last one has let fall a remark
which renewed those doubts of mine when I
read it:

"In our high Parisian existence, for instance, we
find applied to arts and luxury, and to debauchery, all
the powers and all the weaknesses of the French soul."

You see, it amounts to a trade with the
French soul; a profession; a science; the serious business of life, so to speak, in our high
Parisian existence. I do not quite like the
look of it. I question if it can be taught with
profit in our country, except of course to those
pathetic, neglected minds that are waiting
there so yearningly for the education which
M. Bourget is going to furnish them from the
serene summits of our high Parisian life.

I spoke a moment ago of the existence of
some superstitions that have been parading
the world as facts this long time. For instance, consider the Dollar. The world seems

to think that the love of money is "American"; and that the mad desire to get suddenly rich is "American." I believe that both of these things are merely and broadly human, not American monopolies at all. The love of money is natural to all nations, for money is a good and strong friend. I think that this love has existed everywhere, ever since the Bible called it the root of all evil.

I think that the reason why we Americans seem to be so addicted to trying to get rich suddenly is merely because the *opportunity* to make promising efforts in that direction has offered itself to us with a frequency out of all proportion to the European experience. For eighty years this opportunity has been offering itself in one new town or region after another straight westward, step by step, all the way from the Atlantic coast to the Pacific. When a mechanic could buy ten town lots on tolerably long credit for ten months' savings out of his wages, and reasonably expect to sell them in a couple of years for ten times what he gave for them, it was human for him to try the venture, and he did it no matter what his nationality was. He would have done it in Europe or China if he had had the same chance.

In the flush times in the silver regions a cook or any other humble worker stood a very good chance to get rich out of a trifle of money risked in a stock deal; and that person promptly took that risk, no matter what his or her nationality might be. I was there, and saw it.

But these opportunities have not been plenty in our Southern States; so there you have a prodigious region where the rush for sudden wealth is almost an unknown thing—and has been, from the beginning.

Europe has offered few opportunities for poor Tom, Dick, and Harry; but when she has offered one, there has been no noticeable difference between European eagerness and American. England saw this in the wild days of the Railroad King; France saw it in 1720 —time of Law and the Mississippi Bubble. I am sure I have never seen in the gold and silver mines any madness, fury, frenzy to get suddenly rich which was even remotely comparable to that which raged in France in the Bubble day. If I had a cyclopædia here I could turn to that memorable case, and satisfy nearly anybody that the hunger for the sudden dollar is no more " American " than it is French. And if I could furnish an Ameri-

can opportunity to staid Germany, I think I
could wake her up like a house afire.

But I must return to the Generalizations,
Psychologizings, Deductions.   When M. Bourget is exploiting these arts, it is then that
he is peculiarly and particularly himself.   His
ways are wholly original when he encounters a
trait or a custom which is new to him.   Another
person would merely examine the find, verify
it, estimate its value, and let it go; but that is
not sufficient for M. Bourget: he always wants
to know *why* that thing exists, he wants to
know how it came to happen; and he will not
let go of it until he has found out.   And in
every instance he will find that reason where
no one but himself would have thought of
looking for it.   He does not seem to care for
a reason that is not picturesquely located; one
might almost say picturesquely and impossibly
located.

He found out that in America men do not
try to hunt down young married women.   At
once, as usual, he wanted to know *why*.   Any
one could have told him.   He could have
divined it by the lights thrown by the novels
of the country.   But no, he preferred to find
out for himself.   He has a trustfulness as regards men and facts which is fine and unusual;

he is not particular about the source of a fact, he is not particular about the character and standing of the fact itself; but when it comes to pounding out the reason for the existence of the fact, he will trust no one but himself.

In the present instance here was his fact: American young married women are not pursued by the corruptor; and here was the question: What is it that protects her?

It seems quite unlikely that that problem could have offered difficulties to any but a trained philosopher. Nearly any person would have said to M. Bourget: "Oh, that is very simple. It is very seldom in America that a marriage is made on a commercial basis; our marriages, from the beginning, have been made for love; and where love is there is no room for the corruptor."

Now, it is interesting to see the formidable way in which M. Bourget went at that poor, humble little thing. He moved upon it in column—three columns—and with artillery.

"Two reasons of a very different kind explain"—that fact.

And now that I have got so far, I am almost afraid to say what his two reasons are, lest I be charged with inventing them. But I will not retreat now; I will condense them and print them, giving my word that I am honest, and not trying to deceive any one.

1. Young married women are protected from the approaches of the seducer in New England and vicinity by the diluted remains of a prudence created by a Puritan law of two hundred years ago, which for a while punished adultery with death.

2. And young married women of the other forty or fifty States are protected by laws which afford extraordinary facilities for divorce.

If I have not lost my mind I have accurately conveyed those two Vesuvian irruptions of philosophy. But the reader can consult Chapter IV. of *Outre-Mer* and decide for himself. Let us examine this paralyzing Deduction or Explanation by the light of a few sane facts.

1. This universality of "protection" has existed in our country *from the beginning;* before the death penalty existed in New England, and during all the generations that have dragged by since it was annulled.

2. Extraordinary facilities for divorce are of such recent creation that any middle-aged American can remember a time when such things had not yet been thought of.

Let us suppose that the first easy divorce

law went into effect forty years ago, and got noised around and fairly started in business thirty-five years ago, when we had, say, 25,-000,000 of white population. Let us suppose that among 5,000,000 of them the young married women were "protected" by the surviving shudder of that ancient Puritan scare—what is M. Bourget going to do about those who lived among the 20,000,000? They were clean in their morals, they were pure, yet there was no easy divorce law to protect them.

Awhile ago I said that M. Bourget's method of truth-seeking—hunting for it in out-of-the-way places—was new; but that was an error. I remember that when Leverrier discovered the Milky Way, he and the other astronomers began to theorize about it in substantially the same fashion which M. Bourget employs in his reasonings about American social facts and their origin. Leverrier advanced the hypothesis that the Milky Way was caused by gaseous protoplasmic emanations from the field of Waterloo, which, ascending to an altitude determinable by their own specific gravity, became luminous through the development and exposure—by the natural processes of animal decay—of the phosphorus contained in them.

This theory was warmly complimented by

Ptolemy, who, however, after much thought and research, decided that he could not accept it as final. His own theory was that the Milky Way was an emigration of lightning-bugs; and he supported and reinforced this theorem by the well-known fact that the locusts do like that in Egypt.

Giordano Bruno also was outspoken in his praises of Leverrier's important contribution to astronomical science, and was at first inclined to regard it as conclusive; but later, conceiving it to be erroneous, he pronounced against it, and advanced the hypothesis that the Milky Way was a detachment or corps of stars which became arrested and held in *suspenso suspensorum* by refraction of gravitation while on the march to join their several constellations; a proposition for which he was afterwards burned at the stake in Jacksonville, Illinois.

These were all brilliant and picturesque theories, and each was received with enthusiasm by the scientific world; but when a New England farmer, who was not a thinker, but only a plain sort of person who tried to account for large facts in simple ways, came out with the opinion that the Milky Way was just common, ordinary stars, and was put where it was because God "wanted to hev it so," the admirable idea fell perfectly flat.

As a literary artist, M. Bourget is as fresh and striking as he is as a scientific one. He says, "Above all, I do not believe much in anecdotes." Why? "In history they are all false"—a sufficiently broad statement—"in literature all libellous"—also a sufficiently sweeping statement, coming from a critic who notes that we are a people who are peculiarly extravagant in our language—"and when it is a matter of social life, almost all biassed." It seems to amount to stultification, almost. He has built two or three breeds of American coquettes out of anecdotes—mainly "biassed" ones, I suppose; and, as they occur "in literature," furnished by his pen, they must be "all libellous." Or did he mean not *in* literature or anecdotes *about* literature or literary people? I am not able to answer that. Perhaps the original would be clearer, but I have only the translation of this instalment by me. I think the remark had an intention; also that this intention was booked for the trip; but that either in the hurry of the remark's departure it got left, or in the confusion of changing cars at the translator's frontier it got side-tracked.

"But on the other hand I believe in statistics; and those on divorces appear to me to be most conclusive." And he sets himself the task of explaining—in a couple of columns—the process by which Easy-Divorce conceived, invented, originated, developed, and perfected an empire-embracing condition of sexual purity in the States. *In 40 years.* No, he doesn't state the interval. With all his passion for statistics he forgot to ask how long it took to produce this gigantic miracle.

I have followed his pleasant but devious trail through those columns, but I was not able to get hold of his argument and find out what it was. I was not even able to find out where it left off. It seemed to gradually dissolve and flow off into other matters. I followed it with interest, for I was anxious to learn how easy-divorce eradicated adultery in America, but I was disappointed; I have no idea yet how it did it. I only know it didn't. But that is not valuable; I knew it before.

Well, humor is the great thing, the saving thing, after all. The minute it crops up, all our hardnesses yield, all our irritations and resentments flit away, and a sunny spirit takes their place. And so, when M. Bourget said that bright thing about our grandfathers, I

broke all up. I remember exploding its American countermine once, under that grand hero,
Napoleon. He was only First Consul then,
and I was Consul - General — for the United
States, of course; but we were very intimate,
notwithstanding the difference in rank, for I
waived that. One day something offered the
opening, and he said:

"Well, General, I suppose life can never get
entirely dull to an American, because whenever he can't strike up any other way to put
in his time he can always get away with a few
years trying to find out who his grandfather
was!"

I fairly shouted, for I had never heard it
sound better; and then I was back at him as
quick as a flash:

"Right, your Excellency! But I reckon a
Frenchman's got *his* little stand-by for a dull
time, too; because when all other interests fail
he can turn in and see if he can't find out who
his father was!"

Well, you should have heard him just whoop,
and cackle, and carry on! He reached up and
hit me one on the shoulder, and says:

"Land, but it's good! It's im-mensely
good! I'George, I never heard it said so good
in my life before! Say it again."

So I said it again, and he said his again, and
I said mine again, and then he did, and then I
did, and then he did, and we kept on doing it,
and doing it, and I *never* had such a good
time, and he said the same. In my opinion
there isn't anything that is as killing as one of
those dear old ripe pensioners if you know how
to snatch it out in a kind of a fresh sort of
original way.

But I wish M. Bourget had read more of our
novels before he came. It is the only way to
thoroughly understand a people. When I
found I was coming to Paris, I read *La Terre*.

A LITTLE NOTE TO M. PAUL BOURGET

A LITTLE NOTE TO M. PAUL BOURGET

[The preceding squib was assailed in the *North American Review* in an article entitled "Mark Twain and Paul Bourget," by Max O'Rell. The following little note is a Rejoinder to that article. It is possible that the position assumed here—that M. Bourget dictated the O'Rell article himself—is untenable.]

You have every right, my dear M. Bourget, to retort upon me by dictation, if you prefer that method to writing at me with your pen; but if I may say it without hurt—and certainly I mean no offence—I believe you would have acquitted yourself better with the pen. With the pen you are at home; it is your natural weapon; you use it with grace, eloquence, charm, persuasiveness, when men are to be convinced, and with formidable effect when they have earned a castigation. But I am sure I see signs in the above article that you are either unaccustomed to dictating or are out of practice. If you will re-read it you will notice, yourself, that it lacks definiteness; that

it lacks purpose; that it lacks coherence; that
it lacks a subject to talk about; that it is loose
and wabbly; that it wanders around; that it
loses itself early and does not find itself any
more. There are some other defects, as you
will notice, but I think I have named the main
ones. I feel sure that they are all due to your
lack of practice in dictating.

Inasmuch as you had not signed it I had
the impression at first that you had not dictated it. But only for a moment. Certain
quite simple and definite facts reminded me
that the article *had* to come from you, for the
reason that it could not come from any one else
without a specific invitation from you or from
me. I mean, it could not except as an intrusion, a transgression of the law which forbids
strangers to mix into a private dispute between friends, unasked.

Those simple and definite facts were these:
I had published an article in this magazine,
with you for my subject; just you yourself; I
stuck strictly to that one subject, and did not
interlard any other. No one, of course, could
call me to account but you alone, or your authorized representative. I asked some questions — asked them of myself. I answered
them myself. My article was thirteen pages

long, and all devoted to you; devoted to you,
and divided up in this way: one page of
guesses as to what subjects you would instruct
us in, as teacher; one page of doubts as to
the effectiveness of your method of examining
us and our ways; two or three pages of criticism of your method, and of certain results
which it furnished you; two or three pages of
attempts to show the justness of these same
criticisms; half a dozen pages made up of
slight fault-findings with certain minor details
of your literary workmanship, of extracts from
your *Outre-Mer* and comments upon them;
then I closed with an anecdote. I repeat—
for certain reasons—that *I closed with an anecdote.*

When I was asked by this magazine if I
wished to "answer" a "reply" to that article
of mine, I said "yes," and waited in Paris for
the proof-sheets of the "reply" to come. I
already knew, by the cablegram, that the "reply" would not be signed by you, but upon
reflection I knew it would be dictated by you,
because no volunteer would feel himself at
liberty to assume your championship in a private dispute, unasked, in view of the fact that
you are quite well able to take care of your
matters of that sort yourself and are not in

need of any one's help. No, a volunteer could not make such a venture. It would be too immodest. Also too gratuitously generous. And a shade too self-sufficient. No, he could not venture it. It would look like too much anxiety to get in at a feast where no plate had been provided for him. In fact he could not get in at all, except by the back way and with a false key; that is to say, a pretext—a pretext invented for the occasion by putting into my mouth words which I did not use, and by wresting sayings of mine from their plain and true meaning. Would he resort to methods like those to get in? No; there are no people of that kind. So then I knew for a certainty that you dictated the Reply yourself. I knew you did it to save yourself manual labor.

And you had the right, as I have already said; and I am content—perfectly content. Yet it would have been little trouble to you, and a great kindness to me, if you had written your Reply all out with your own capable hand.

Because then it would have replied—and that is really what a Reply is for. Broadly speaking, its function is to refute—as you will easily concede. That leaves something for the other person to take hold of: he has a chance to reply to the Reply, he has a chance to refute the refutation. This would have happened if you had written it out instead of dictating. Dictating is nearly sure to unconcentrate the dictator's mind, when he is out of practice, confuse him, and betray him into using one set of literary rules when he ought to use a quite different set. Often it betrays him into employing the RULES FOR CONVERSATION BETWEEN A SHOUTER AND A DEAF PERSON—as in the present case—when he ought to employ the RULES FOR CONDUCTING DISCUSSION WITH A FAULT-FINDER. The great foundation-rule and basic principle of discussion with a fault-finder is relevancy and concentration upon the subject; whereas the great foundation-rule and basic principle governing conversation between a shouter and a deaf person is irrelevancy and persistent desertion of the topic in hand. If I may be allowed to illustrate by quoting example IV., section 7, from chapter ix. of "Revised Rules for Conducting Conversation between a Shouter and a Deaf Person," it will assist us in getting a clear idea of the difference between the two sets of rules:

Shouter. Did you say his name is WETHERBY?

Deaf Person. Change? Yes, I think it will. Though if it should clear off I—

Shouter. It's his NAME I want—his NAME.

Deaf Person. Maybe so, maybe so; but it will only be a shower, I think.

Shouter. No, no, *no!*—you have quite mis-underSTOOD me. If—

Deaf Person. Ah! GOOD morning; I am sorry you must go. But call again, and let me continue to be of assistance to you in every way I can.

You see, it is a perfect kodak of the article you have dictated. It is really curious and interesting when you come to compare it with yours; in detail, with my former article to which it is a Reply in your hand. I talk twelve pages about your American instruction projects, and your doubtful scientific system, and your painstaking classification of non-existent things, and your diligence and zeal and sincerity, and your disloyal attitude towards anecdotes, and your undue reverence for unsafe statistics and for facts that lack a pedigree; and you turn around and come back at me with eight pages of weather.

I do not see how a person can act so. It is good of you to repeat, with change of language, in the bulk of your rejoinder, so much of my own article, and adopt my sentiments, and make them over, and put new buttons on; and I like the compliment, and am frank to say so; but *agreeing* with a person cripples controversy and ought not to be allowed. It is weather; and of almost the worst sort. It pleases me greatly to hear you discourse with such approval and expansiveness upon my text:

"A foreigner can photograph the exteriors of a nation, but I think that is as far as he can get. I think that no foreigner can report its interior;"* which is a quite clear way of saying that a foreigner's report is only valuable when it restricts itself to *impressions*. It pleases me to have you follow my lead in that glowing way, but it leaves me nothing to combat. You should give me something to deny and refute; I would do as much for you.

It pleases me to have you playfully warn the public against taking one of your books

---

*And you say: "A man of average intelligence, who has passed six months among a people, cannot express opinions that are worth jotting down, but he can form impressions that are worth repeating. For my part, I think that foreigners' impressions are more interesting than native opinions. After all, such impressions merely mean 'how the country *struck* the foreigner.'"

seriously.*   Because I used to do that cunning thing myself in earlier days.   I did it in a prefatory note to a book of mine called *Tom Sawyer*.

NOTICE

Persons attempting to find a motive in this narrative will be prosecuted; persons attempting to find a moral in it will be banished; persons attempting to find a plot in it will be shot.

BY ORDER OF THE AUTHOR
PER G. G., CHIEF OF ORDNANCE.

The kernel is the same in both prefaces, you see—the public must not take us too seriously. If we remove that kernel we remove the life-principle, and the preface is a corpse.   Yes, it pleases me to have you use that idea, for it is a high compliment.   But it leaves me nothing to combat; and that is damage to me.

Am I seeming to say that your Reply is not a reply at all, M. Bourget?   If so, I must modify that; it is too sweeping.   For you have furnished a general answer to my inquiry as

---

* When I published *Jonathan and his Continent*, I wrote in a preface addressed to Jonathan: "If ever you should insist in seeing in this little volume a serious study of your country and of your countrymen, I warn you that your world-wide fame for humor will be exploded."

to what France—through you—can teach us.*
It is a good answer.   It relates to manners,
customs, and morals — three things concerning which we can never have exhaustive and
determinate statistics, and so the verdicts de-

---

* " What could France teach America ?" exclaims Mark
Twain.   France can teach America all the higher pursuits of
life, and there is more artistic feeling and refinement in a
street of French working-men than in many avenues inhabited
by American millionaires.   She can teach her, not perhaps
how to work, but how to rest, how to live, how to be happy.
She can teach her that the aim of life is not money-making,
but that money-making is only a means to obtain an end.
She can teach her that wives are not expensive toys, but useful partners, friends, and confidants, who should always keep
men under their wholesome influence by their diplomacy,
their tact, their common-sense, without bumptiousness.   These
qualities, added to the highest standard of morality (not an-
gular and morose, but cheerful morality), are conceded to
Frenchwomen by whoever knows something of French life
outside of the Paris boulevards, and Mark Twain's ill-natured
sneer can not even so much as stain them.

I might tell Mark Twain that in France a man who was
seen tipsy in his club would immediately see his name can-
celled from membership.   A man who had settled his fortune
on his wife to avoid meeting his creditors would be refused
admission into any decent society.   Many a Frenchman has
blown his brains out rather than declare himself a bankrupt.
Now would Mark Twain remark to this : " An American is
not such a fool : when a creditor stands in his way he closes
his doors, and reopens them the following day.   When he
has been a bankrupt three times he can retire from business ?"

livered upon them must always lack conclu-
siveness and be subject to revision; but you
have stated the truth, possibly, as nearly as
any one could do it, in the circumstances. But
why did you choose a detail of my question
which could be answered only with vague
hearsay evidence, and go right by one which
could have been answered with deadly facts?
—facts in everybody's reach, facts which none
can dispute. I asked what France could teach
us about government. I laid myself pretty
wide open, there; and I thought I was handsomely generous, too, when I did it. France
can teach us how to levy village and city taxes
which distribute the burden with a nearer approach to perfect fairness than is the case in
any other land; and she can teach us the wis-
est and surest system of collecting them that
exists. She can teach us how to elect a President in a sane way; and also how to do it
without throwing the country into earthquakes
and convulsions that cripple and embarrass
business, stir up party hatred in the hearts of
men, and make peaceful people wish the term
extended to thirty years. France can teach
us—but enough of that part of the question.
And what else can France teach us? She can
teach us all the fine arts — and does. She

throws open her hospitable art academies, and says to us, "Come"—and we come, troops and troops of our young and gifted; and she sets over us the ablest masters in the world and bearing the greatest names; and she teaches us all that we are capable of learning, and persuades us and encourages us with prizes and honors, much as if we were somehow children of her own; and when this noble education is finished and we are ready to carry it home and spread its gracious ministries abroad over our nation, and we come with homage and gratitude and ask France for the bill—*there is nothing to pay*. And in return for this imperial generosity, what does America do? She charges a duty on French works of art!

I wish I had your end of this dispute; I should have something worth talking about. If you would only furnish me something to argue, something to refute—but you persistently won't. You leave good chances unutilized and spend your strength in proving and establishing unimportant things. For instance, you have proven and established these eight facts here following—a good score as to number, but not worth while:

Mark Twain is—

1. "Insulting."

2. (Sarcastically speaking) '' This refined humorist."

3. Prefers the manure-pile to the violets.

4. Has uttered " an ill-natured sneer."

5. Is " nasty."

6. Needs a " lesson in politeness and good manners."

7. Has published a " nasty article."

8. Has made remarks "unworthy of a gentleman." *

These are all true, but really they are not valuable ; no one cares much for such finds. In our American magazines we recognize this and suppress them. We avoid naming them. American writers never allow themselves to

---

* " It is more funny than his " (Mark Twain's) " anecdote, and would have been less insulting."

A quoted remark of mine " is a gross insult to a nation friendly to America."

" He has read *La Terre*, this refined humorist."

" When Mark Twain visits a garden . . . he goes in the far-away corner where the soil is prepared."

" Mark Twain's ill-natured sneer cannot so much as stain them " (the Frenchwomen).

" When he " (Mark Twain) " takes his revenge he is unkind, unfair, bitter, nasty."

" But not even your nasty article on my country, Mark," etc.

" Mark might certainly have derived from it " (M. Bourget's book) " a lesson in politeness and good manners."

A quoted remark of mine is " unworthy of a gentleman."

name them.   It would look as if they were in
a temper, and we hold that exhibitions of
temper in public are not good form—except
in the very young and inexperienced.   And
even if we had the disposition to name them,
in order to fill up a gap when we were short
of ideas and arguments, our magazines would
not allow us to do it, because they think that
such words sully their pages.   This present
magazine is particularly strenuous about it.
Its note to me announcing the forwarding of
your proof-sheets to France closed thus—for
your protection:

" *It is needless to ask you to avoid anything
that he might consider as personal.*"

It was well enough, as a measure of pre-
caution, but really it was not needed.   You
can trust me implicitly, M. Bourget; I shall
never call you any names in print which I
should be ashamed to call you with your unoffending and dearest ones present.

Indeed, we are reserved, and particular in
America to a degree which you would consider exaggerated.   For instance, we should
not write notes like that one of yours to a
lady for a small fault—or a large one.*   We

* When M. Paul Bourget indulges in a little chaffing at
the expense of the Americans, "who can always get away

should not think it kind. No matter how much we might have associated with kings and nobilities, we should not think it right to crush her with it and make her ashamed

with a few years' trying to find out who their grandfathers were," he merely makes an allusion to an American foible ; but, forsooth, what a kind man, what a humorist Mark Twain is when he retorts by calling France a nation of bastards ! How the Americans of culture and refinement will admire him for thus speaking in their name !

Snobbery. . . . I could give Mark Twain an example of the American specimen. It is a piquant story. I never published it because I feared my readers might think that I was giving them a typical illustration of American character instead of a rare exception.

I was once booked by my manager to give a *causerie* in the drawing-room of a New York millionaire. I accepted with reluctance. I do not like private engagements. At five o'clock on the day the *causerie* was to be given, the lady sent to my manager to say that she would expect me to arrive at nine o'clock and to speak for about an hour. Then she wrote a postscript. Many women are unfortunate there. Their minds are full of after-thoughts, and the most important part of their letters is generally to be found after their signature. This lady's P. S. ran thus: "I suppose he will not expect to be entertained after the lecture."

I fairly shouted, as Mark Twain would say, and then, indulging myself in a bit of snobbishness, I was back at her as quick as a flash—

"Dear Madam: As a literary man of some reputation, I have many times had the pleasure of being entertained by the members of the old aristocracy of France. I have also many

of her lowlier walk in life; for we have a saying, "Who humiliates my mother includes his
own."

Do I seriously imagine you to be the author of that strange letter, M. Bourget? Indeed I do not. I believe it to have been
surreptitiously inserted by your amanuensis
when your back was turned. I think he did it
with a good motive, expecting it to add force
and piquancy to your article, but it does not
reflect your nature, and I know it will grieve
you when you see it. I also think he inter-
larded many other things which you will dis-
approve of when you see them. I am certain
that all the harsh names discharged at me

times had the pleasure of being entertained by the members
of the old aristocracy of England. If it may interest you, I
can even tell you that I have several times had the honor of
being entertained by royalty; but my ambition has never
been so wild as to expect that one day I might be entertained
by the aristocracy of New York. No, I do not expect to be
entertained by you, nor do I want you to expect me to en-
tertain you and your friends to-night, for I decline to keep
the engagement."

Now, I could fill a book on America with reminiscences of
this sort, adding a few chapters on bosses and boodlers, on
New York *chronique scandaleuse*, on the tenement houses
of the large cities, on the gambling-hells of Denver, and the
dens of San Francisco, and what not! But not even your
nasty article on my country, Mark, will make me do it.

come from him, not you. No doubt you could have proved me entitled to them with as little trouble as it has cost him to do it, but it would have been your disposition to hunt game of a higher quality.

Why, I even doubt if it is you who furnish me all that excellent information about Balzac and those others.* All this in simple justice to you—and to me; for, to gravely accept those interlardings as yours would be to wrong your head and heart, and at the same time

---

* " Now the style of M. Bourget and many other French writers is apparently a closed letter to Mark Twain; but let us leave that alone. Has he read Erckmann-Chatrian, Victor Hugo, Lamartine, Edmond About, Cherbuliez, Renan? Has he read Gustave Droz's *Monsieur, Madame, et Bébé*, and those books which leave for a long time a perfume about you? Has he read the novels of Alexandre Dumas, Eugène Sue, George Sand, and Balzac? Has he read Victor Hugo's *Les Misérables* and *Notre Dame de Paris?* Has he read or heard the plays of Sandeau, Augier, Dumas, and Sardou, the works of those Titans of modern literature, whose names will be household words all over the world for hundreds of years to come? He has read *La Terre*—this kind-hearted, refined humorist! When Mark Twain visits a garden does he smell the violets, the roses, the jasmine, or the honeysuckle? No, he goes in the far-away corner where the soil is prepared. Hear what he says: "I wish M. Paul Bourget had read more of our novels before he came. It is the only way to thoroughly understand a people. When I found I was coming to Paris I read *La Terre*."

convict myself of being equipped with a va-
cancy where my penetration ought to be
lodged.

And now finally I must uncover the secret
pain, the wee sore from which the Reply grew
—*the anecdote which closed my recent article*—
and consider how it is that this pimple has
spread to these cancerous dimensions. If any
but you had dictated the Reply, M. Bourget,
I would know that that anecdote was twisted
around and its intention magnified some hundreds of times, in order that it might be used
as a pretext to creep in the back way. But
I accuse you of nothing—nothing but error.
When you say that I "retort by calling France
a nation of bastards," it is an error. And not
a small one, but a large one. I made no such
remark, nor anything resembling it. Moreover, the magazine would not have allowed
me to use so gross a word as that.

You told an anecdote. A funny one — I
admit that. It hit a foible of our American
aristocracy, and it stung me—I admit that;
it stung me sharply. It was like this: You
found some ancient portraits of French kings
in the gallery of one of our aristocracy, and
you said:

"He has the Grand Monarch, but *where is*

the portrait of his grandfather ?" That is, the American aristocrat's grandfather.

Now that hits only a few of us, I grant— just the upper crust only—but it hits exceedingly hard.

I wondered if there was any way of getting back at you. In one of your chapters I found this chance:

"In our high Parisian existence, for instance, we find applied to arts and luxury, and to debauchery, all the powers and all the weaknesses of the French soul."

You see? Your " higher Parisian" class— not everybody, not the nation, but only the *top crust* of the nation—*applies to debauchery all the powers of its soul.*

I argued to myself that that energy must produce results. So I built an anecdote out of your remark. In it I make Napoleon Bonaparte say to me — but see for yourself the anecdote (ingeniously clipped and curtailed) in paragraph eleven of your Reply.*

* So, I repeat, Mark Twain does not like M. Paul Bourget's book. So long as he makes light fun of the great French writer he is at home, he is pleasant, he is the American humorist we know. When he takes his revenge (and where is the reason for taking a revenge ?) he is unkind, unfair, bitter, nasty.

Now then, your anecdote about the grand-fathers hurt me. Why? Because it had *point*. It wouldn't have hurt me if it hadn't had point. You wouldn't have wasted space on it if it hadn't had point.

My anecdote has hurt you. Why? Be-

For example :

See his answer to a Frenchman who jokingly remarks to him :

" I suppose life can never get entirely dull to an American, because whenever he can't strike up any other way to put in his time, he can always get away with a few years trying to find out who his grandfather was."

Hear the answer :

" I reckon a Frenchman's got *his* little standby for a dull time, too ; because when all other interests fail, he can turn in and see if he can't find out who his father was ?"

The first remark is a good-humored bit of chaffing on American snobbery. I may be utterly destitute of humor, but I call the second remark a gratuitous charge of immoral-ity hurled at the French women—a remark unworthy of a man who has the ear of the public, unworthy of a gentleman, a gross insult to a nation friendly to America, a nation that helped Mark Twain's ancestors in their struggle for liberty, a nation where to-day it is enough to say that you are American to see every door open wide to you.

If Mark Twain was hard up in search of a French " chest-nut," I might have told him the following little anecdote. It is more funny than his, and would have been less insulting : Two little street boys are abusing each other. " Ah, hold your tongue," says one, " you ain't got no father."

" Ain't got no father !" replies the other ; " I've got more fathers than you."

cause it had point, I suppose. It wouldn't
have hurt you if it hadn't had point. I judged
from your remark about the diligence and
industry of the high Parisian upper crust that
it would have *some* point, but really I had no
idea what a gold-mine I had struck. I never
suspected that the point was going to stick into
the entire nation ; but of course you know your
nation better than I do, and if you think it punct-
ures them all, I have to yield to your judgment.
But you are to blame, your own self. Your remark misled me. I supposed the industry was
confined to that little unnumerous upper layer.

Well, now that the unfortunate thing has
been done, let us do what we can to undo it.
There must be a way, M. Bourget, and I am
willing to do anything that will help ; for I am
as sorry as you can be yourself.

I will tell you what I think will be the very
thing. We will *swap anecdotes*. I will take
your anecdote and you take mine. I will say
to the dukes and counts and princes of the
ancient nobility of France : " Ha, ha ! You
must have a pretty hard time trying to find
out who your grandfathers were ?"

They will merely smile indifferently and
not feel hurt, because they can trace their
lineage back through centuries.

And you will hurl mine at every individual in the American nation, saying:

"And *you* must have a pretty hard time trying to find out who your *fathers* were."

They will merely smile indifferently, and not feel hurt, because they haven't any difficulty in finding their fathers.

Do you get the idea? The whole harm in the anecdotes is in the *point*, you see; and when we swap them around that way, they *haven't* any.

That settles it perfectly and beautifully, and I am glad I thought of it. I am very glad indeed, M. Bourget; for it was just that little wee thing that caused the whole difficulty and made you dictate the Reply, and your aman- uensis call me all those hard names which the magazines dislike so. And I did it all in fun, too, trying to cap your funny anecdote with another one—on the give-and-take principle, you know—which is American. *I* didn't know that with the French it was all give and no take, and you didn't tell me. But now that I have made everything comfortable again, and fixed both anecdotes so they can never have any point any more, I know you will forgive me.

THE END

HARPER'S AMERICAN ESSAYISTS

OTHER TIMES AND OTHER SEASONS. By LAU-
RENCE HUTTON.

A LITTLE ENGLISH GALLERY. By LOUISE IMO-
GEN GUINEY.

LITERARY AND SOCIAL SILHOUETTES. By
HJALMAR HJORTH BOYESEN.

STUDIES OF THE STAGE. By BRANDER MATTHEWS.

AMERICANISMS AND BRITICISMS, with Other Essays on Other Isms. By BRANDER MATTHEWS.

AS WE GO. By CHARLES DUDLEY WARNER. With
Illustrations.

AS WE WERE SAYING. By CHARLES DUDLEY
WARNER. With Illustrations.

FROM THE EASY CHAIR. By GEORGE WILLIAM
CURTIS.

FROM THE EASY CHAIR. *Second Series.* By GEORGE
WILLIAM CURTIS.

FROM THE EASY CHAIR. *Third Series.* By GEORGE
WILLIAM CURTIS.

CRITICISM AND FICTION. By WILLIAM DEAN
HOWELLS.

FROM THE BOOKS OF LAURENCE HUTTON.

CONCERNING ALL OF US. By THOMAS WENT-
WORTH HIGGINSON.

THE WORK OF JOHN RUSKIN. By CHARLES
WALDSTEIN.

PICTURE AND TEXT. By HENRY JAMES. With
Illustrations.

16mo, Cloth, $1 00 each. Complete Sets, in White and Gold,
$1 25 a Volume.

PUBLISHED BY HARPER & BROTHERS, NEW YORK.

☞ *The above works are for sale by all booksellers, or will be mailed by
the publishers, postage prepaid, on receipt of the price.*

By GEORGE DU MAURIER

ENGLISH SOCIETY. Sketched by GEORGE DU
MAURIER. About 100 Illustrations. With an Intro-
duction by W. D. HOWELLS. Oblong 4to, Cloth,
Ornamental, $2 50.

A volume which it will always be a delight to have in the
house. In it a searching observer of many phases of humanity, charming in its wit and without the blemish of malice,
presents with his pencil as much of his social philosophy as
he could give with his pen in a hundred novels.—*N. Y. Sun.*

As to the drawings, what can we say in praise of them that
has not been said time and again ? The humor, the satire, so
effective notwithstanding the light touch, are all here, as they
are in everything that Du Maurier drew.—*Critic,* N. Y.

TRILBY. A Novel. Illustrated by the Author. Post
8vo, Cloth, Ornamental, $1 75 ; Three-quarter Calf,
$3 50 ; Three-quarter Crushed Levant, $4 50.

Mr. Du Maurier has written his tale with such originality,
unconventionality, and eloquence, such rollicking humor and
tender pathos, and delightful play of every lively fancy, all
running so briskly in exquisite English, and with such vivid
dramatic picturing, that it is only comparable . . . to the
freshness and beauty of a spring morning at the end of a
dragging winter. . . . A thoroughly unique story.—*N. Y. Sun.*

PETER IBBETSON. With an Introduction by his
Cousin, Lady * * * * ("Madge Plunket"). Edited
and Illustrated by GEORGE DU MAURIER. Post 8vo,
Cloth, Ornamental, $1 50 ; Three-quarter Calf, $3 25;
Three-quarter Crushed Levant, $4 25.

There are so many beauties, so many singularities, so much
that is fresh and original, in Mr. Du Maurier's story that it is
difficult to treat it at all adequately from the point of view of
criticism. That it is one of the most remarkable books that
have appeared for a long time is, however, indisputable.—
N. Y. Tribune.

PUBLISHED BY HARPER & BROTHERS, NEW YORK.

☞ *The above works are for sale by all booksellers, or will be mailed by
the publishers, postage prepaid, on receipt of the price.*

AFTERWORD

Pascal Covici, Jr.

When he wrote the essays in this volume, Mark Twain was going through some of his most painful experiences. In June of 1891, the Clemens family closed up their Hartford, Connecticut, home of almost twenty years and tried to economize by living in Europe. The dollars that had long been poured hopefully into the Paige typesetting machine had drained the family's resources. Finally, with the failure of Charles L. Webster and Company, the publishing house with which Mark Twain had closely allied himself, America's beloved author declared bankruptcy in April of 1894. When *Pudd'nhead Wilson* appeared later that year, reviewers sneered at the book and at its author, as much for the latter's fiscal failure as for the former's alleged artistic insufficiencies. But then, by the end of the 1898–99 winter, he had paid all his debts, sparing his family, and especially his wife, considerable shame, but driving himself unmercifully in the process. The family fortunes having been restructured with the astute help of H. H. Rogers of the Standard Oil Company, Twain's money troubles were over. Mark Twain even became something of a national hero by making good on his pledge to pay one hundred cents on the dollar. Legally, he could have taken a much easier way, but he chose not to do so. The public approbation, however, came after this collection of essays first appeared.

The 1890s took a harsh toll: in addition to the bankruptcy, not only did his wife's health continue to fail — Livy would die in June of 1904 — but his favorite daughter, Susy, died in August of 1896, while he and Livy and their daughter Clara were abroad. Harper's publication in 1897 of *How to Tell a Story and Other Essays* was an important part of Twain's financial reconstruction, but the author was in no mood to celebrate when the volume came out. Readers' pleasure in its contents seems ironic when one considers Twain's feelings of anxiety, shame, grief, and guilt while he was producing these pieces. What counts, finally, is that the work got done: we have it, and we can revel in the facets of himself that Twain reveals or else hides imperfectly from view.

"How to Tell a Story," the title piece, appeared originally in *Youth's Companion* in October 1895. In a small nutshell, and in very simple terms that imply an intuitive and imitative, rather than an analytic, approach, Twain here pins down three elements that characterize his own work, elements significant not only to his stylistic effects but to the very meaning of his whole literary enterprise. Whether retreating into silence for a pregnant and perfectly timed pause, or presenting himself in deadpan pseudo-innocence (lacking in whatever affect the situation might seem to demand), or disappearing from view behind the mask of a deliberately contrived performance, the author uses these three elements — the pause, the poker face, the pretended identity (8–9) — to create a world that undercuts, at times attacks, the world of everyday by forcing readers to experience and to examine what they know from a perspective that is not habitual to them.

At times, this perspective creates amusement only. For example, consider Twain the performer as he struggled to perfect his delivery of Jim Blaine's story of his grandfather's ram — one of the hilarious set pieces in *Roughing It* — from the lecture platform. Looking back on the process, he discovered that over the months his platform version had come to differ greatly from the printed version. He put the platform text into his autobiography, and remarked:

> I never knew how considerable the changes had been when I finished the season's work; I never knew until ten or eleven years later, when I took up . . . the platform form of the story. . . . Upon comparing the above with the original in *Roughing It*, I find myself unable to clearly and definitely explain why the one can be effectively *recited* before an audience and the

other can't; . . . I sense it but cannot express it; . . . I merely know that the one version will recite, and the other won't.[1]

"I sense it but cannot express it." But the Twain who had written "How to Tell a Story" some dozen years before expressed it very well when he presented the three main elements of the "humorous story." Telling does differ from writing, hearing from reading; and Twain's discussion here of the humorous story makes clear that it is a story told, or written as if told. It is the speaking voice, above all else, that makes this sort of story so pointedly and exclusively an "American art" (8).

On the lecture platform, Twain did what he had not done in *Roughing It*: he himself became Jim Blaine, perfectly drunk, "symmetrically drunk," and possessed of an unforgiving memory that could not distinguish between the tedious and the entertaining. Before telling the story to his audiences, Twain would announce that "the idea of the tale" he was about to present was

> to exhibit the bad effects of a good memory . . . which . . . retards the progress of a narrative, at the same time making a tangled, inextricable confusion of it and intolerably wearisome to the listener. The historian of "His Grandfather's Ram" had that kind of a memory. . . . he always got further and further from his grandfather's memorable adventure with the ram, and finally went to sleep before he got to the end of the story, and so did his comrades.

Then, as Blaine, Twain would begin the story this way:

> Well, as I was a-sayin', he bought that old ram from a feller up in Siskiyou County and fetched him home and turned him loose in the medder, and next morning he went down to have a look at him, and accident'ly dropped a ten-cent piece in the grass and stooped down — so [note the necessity for the platform artist to act out the search] — and was a-fumblin' around in the grass to get it, and the ram he was a-standin' up the slope taking notice; but my grandfather wasn't taking notice, because he had his back to the

ram and was int'rested about the dime. Well, there he was, as I was a-sayin', down at the foot of the slope a-bendin' over — so — fumblin' in the grass, and the ram he was up there at the top of the slope, and Smith — Smith was a standin' there — no, not jest there, a little further away — fifteen foot perhaps — well, my grandfather was a stoopin' way down — so — and the ram was up there observing, you know, and Smith he . . . (musing) . . . the ram he bent his head down, so . . . Smith of Calaveras . . . no, no it couldn't ben Smith of Calaveras — I remember now that he — b'George it was Smith of Tulare County — course it was, I remember it now perfectly plain.

Well, Smith he stood just there, and my grandfather he stood just here, you know, and he was a-bending' down just so, fumblin' in the grass, and when the old ram see him in that attitude he took it fur an invitation — and here he come! down the slope thirty mile an hour and his eye full of business. You see my grandfather's back being to him, and him stooping down like that, of course he — why sho! it *warn't* Smith of Tulare at all, it was Smith of Sacramento — my goodness, how did I ever come to get them Smiths mixed like that — why, Smith of Tulare was jest a nobody, but Smith of Sacramento — why, the Smiths of Sacramento come of the best Southern blood in the United States; there warn't ever any better blood south of the line than the Sacramento Smiths. Why look here, one of them married a Whitaker! I reckon that gives you an idea of the kind of society the Sacramento Smiths could 'sociate around in; there ain't no better blood than that Whitaker blood; I reckon anybody'll tell you that.

And that's the last we hear of the ram, and of the seat of Grandfather's pants, too. Any interest in the intersection of those two fascinating objects is our responsibility, for we have been warned that Jim Blaine's memory will carry him — and therefore us — far away from his initial focus. We have been fooled into hankering after an account of a violent conjunction that can occur only in our own sensation-seeking imaginations; we have only ourselves to blame.

In *Roughing It* (ch. 53), with a different kind of victimization in the author's mind, the story works differently. On the platform, Twain became Jim, whereas in the book he is tricked by "the boys" into listening eagerly to a fascinating story that Jim Blaine would tell only when properly drunk, a story that . . . but here is how Twain the author has Jim begin it in the book:

> I don't reckon them times will ever come again. There never was a more bullier old ram than what he was. Grandfather fetched him from Illinois — got him of a man by the name of Yates — Bill Yates — maybe you might have heard of him; his father was a deacon — Baptist — and he was a rustler, too; a man had to get up ruther early to get the start of old Thankful Yates; it was him that put the Greens up to jining teams with my grandfather when he moved west. Seth Green was prob'ly the pick of the flock; he married a Wilkerson — Sarah Wilkerson — good cretur, she was — one of the likeliest heifers that was ever raised in old Stoddard, everybody said that knowed her.

By the time Jim Blaine falls asleep, having meandered all over the genealogical map without ever returning to the wonderful ram,

> tears were running down the boys' cheeks — they were suffocating with suppressed laughter — and had been from the start, though I had never noticed it. I perceived that I was "sold." . . . What the thing was that happened to him and his grandfather's old ram is a dark mystery to this day, for nobody has ever yet found out.

So ends the chapter, with the reader occupying the same position supposedly occupied by young Twain.

Poker face and performance are devices calculated to deceive, but what about the pause? As illustrated by Twain's account of "The Golden Arm" (9–12), the pause might seem more appropriate to Halloween than to humor. But consider the courtroom scene at the end of *Tom Sawyer, Detective*: just before unraveling the mystery that threatens to send his Uncle Silas to jail for life, Tom Sawyer "stood there and waited a second or two — that was for to work up an 'effect,' as he calls it — then he started in just as ca'm as ever. . . ." The pause works its magic on the crowded courtroom, and it works a different magic on us readers, leading us to chuckle over Tom's triumph.

And then there is the pause as it delivers a moral rather than a humorous punch, the pause that deceives by encouraging readers to look in one direction rather than another. Because readers of *Pudd'nhead Wilson* know all the facts prior to the courtroom scene at the end of the story, the question becomes one not of "who dunit" but of how Wilson will reveal the truth and of what the effects of that revelation will be. As Wilson explains the theory of fingerprinting — anachronistically, to be sure, because the scene is set almost forty years before fingerprinting was seen to have forensic utility — all present have been testing his assertions by looking at their own hands. Then, the pause:

> Wilson stopped and stood silent. Inattention dies a quick and sure death when a speaker does that. The stillness gives warning that something is coming. All palms and finger-balls went down, now, all slouching forms straightened, all heads came up, all eyes were fastened upon Wilson's face. He waited yet one, two, three moments, to let his pause complete and perfect its spell upon the house ...

"Its spell upon the house": precisely. Tom Sawyer the detective, Mark Twain from the lecture platform, Wilson in the courtroom: each one "plays the house." The skillful author uses the pause, but the effects of Wilson's dramatic presentation are complex, and certainly not humorous; instead, they lead readers to an empathy with Wilson, who finally wins the approval, even adulation, of the townsfolk of Dawson's Landing, and thence to an unthinking and untenable glorification of Wilson's exposure of the one-thirty-second-part "black" Tom Driscoll.

Twain, here as elsewhere, uses one or more of the innocent devices of "the humorous story" — here, the pause — to force his reader into a false position. And this is a common practice with him. For instance, at the end of *Huckleberry Finn*, readers condemn the society that prefers theatrical excitement to truth; but we also believe that Tom Sawyer, representative par excellence of that society, will violate its most stringent commandment by freeing a slave. Tom's poker-faced lying, Tom's performance as principled upholder of the ridiculous conventions of sensationalistic literature, and Tom's open-ended pause after almost giving his hand away with his spontaneous "What!

Why, Jim is — ," withholding just in time the word "free": all conspire against us. Similarly, as we read about the society into which David "Pudd'nhead" Wilson comes, we condemn the arbitrary categorizing of human beings as "free" and "slave," "white" and "black," on the basis of an accounting system that maximizes the number of slaves; later, we likewise condemn the judicial system that supports the enslavement of human beings by human beings. But at the end of the book, Twain forces us, however briefly, to sanction those two systems when, as a result of Wilson's triumph, Tom Driscoll — the "real" Chambers and also the "real" slave and murderer — is sold down the river. A reader who has been made to admire Pudd'nhead Wilson cannot help but be "glad" that Wilson succeeds in restoring "order" to the racial and criminal chaos that Roxana and her son have wrought, even though that "order" is based on two of society's most repressive exploitations, racism and slavery. We, too, have a capacity for perversity.

Twain will take this simple trick of the hoax, of putting the reader into a false position, and he will develop it, finally, into a whole metaphysics that calls into question the reality, the very existence, of the universe in which his characters live. This metaphysical experiment, developed in later work,[2] lies buried, perhaps concealed even from Twain's own view, in "How to Tell a Story." This little essay, we might say, anticipates, even explains, the most profound effects of Twain's art, and not simply the delightful humor that perpetually endears him to his readers. And notice how simply, how folksily, Twain does it: "And mind you look out for the pause and get it right" (10), he warns us — as if the intuitive response of the entertainer were his total concern and any more weighty effect beyond his imagining.

In another important essay on literary matters, Twain once again masks complex motives, this time in a seemingly straightforward indignation at broken rules. "Fenimore Cooper's Literary Offences" first appeared in the prestigious, conservative, and stately *North American Review* in July 1895. As befits the solemnity of this official organ of the established culture, Twain purports to be taking Cooper to task for committing, "in the restricted space of two-thirds of a page [of *The Deerslayer*], . . . 114 offences against literary art out of a possible 115," and of having violated, in the course of the same book, eighteen out of a possible "nineteen rules governing literary art in the domain of romantic fiction" (94). Twain pretends to be so concerned with the academic notion that rules do govern "literary art" that he even acknowledges that some authorities would insist upon twenty-two rather than a mere nineteen. This sanctioning of a perspective from which "rules" of literary art take precedence over the intuitive upwellings from a writer's unconscious seems very strange indeed to be coming from Mark Twain, proponent of the hydraulic theory of literary composition. As far back as the writing of *The Adventures of Tom Sawyer*,

> [w]hen the manuscript had lain in a pigeonhole two years . . . I made the great discovery that when the tank runs dry you've only to leave it alone and it will fill up again in time, while you are asleep — also while you are at work at other things and are quite unaware that this unconscious and profitable cerebration is going on. There was plenty of material now and the book went on and finished itself without any trouble.[3]

"Without any trouble": Twain just let the accumulated pressure swash the story out of him, he seems to be saying, with no concern for any of the "rules" governing "literary art." No: what Twain really objects to in Cooper is a little more complicated than Cooper's violation of simple rules, and also more connected to life.

Twain, let us remember, claims to base his attack on one particular sort of "rules," those "governing literary art in the domain of romantic fiction." It's in this "domain" that one finds the clue to what he is really up to. In the early nineteenth century, the great creator of romantic fiction was assuredly Sir Walter Scott. In *Pudd'nhead Wilson* (and elsewhere) Twain names a foolishly sentimental and socially impressionable young thing "Rowena," after the "niminy-piminy" (not his term but that of Scott's critics) heroine of *Ivanhoe*. In chapter 46 of *Life on the Mississippi*, Twain launched a fierce attack on Sir Walter Scott as the man who, through his fiction, was "in great measure responsible" for the Civil War by having had so ruinous an effect on "Southern character, as it existed before the war." More important for understanding why he is gunning for Cooper, Twain held Scott responsible, too, for the postwar continuation of "maudlin Middle-Age romanticism here in the midst of the plainest and sturdiest and infinitely greatest and worthiest of all the centuries the world has seen." The chapter ends with a quick "exemplification of the power of a single book for good or harm . . . in the effects wrought by *Don Quixote* and those wrought by *Ivanhoe*." Whereas Cervantes' early-seventeenth-century masterpiece, in Twain's perhaps skewed view, had "swept the world's admiration for the medieval chivalry-silliness out of existence," Scott's 1819 romance "restored it." This restoration, Twain believed, did the western world immense harm, nowhere more obviously than in the American South.

Cooper, often referred to as "the American Scott," presented in his Leatherstocking tales not simply a world within which combat often follows the patterns set down by Scott — as in the encounter between chivalrous Hard Heart and deceitful Mahtoree toward the end of *The Prairie* — but also a world wherein the ideality of the romantic imagination overwhelms, indeed hides from a reader's consciousness, the scruffy facts of material reality. When Twain objects to Cooper's presentation of the literally incredible efficacy of Natty's marksmanship, the real issue certainly can be articulated as "Cooper's high talent for inaccurate observation," but for us to understand what Twain means requires a somewhat broader paraphrase. We have to take Twain very literally indeed: he means that Cooper does have a *very* "high talent," a talent that leads him to present human experience and humanity not as they appear to careful observers but rather as they might appear in a romanticized, an idealized, picture of what one might wishfully imagine them to be if one were constructing a Platonic model of Ideal Forms, or in mid-nineteenth-century terms, an image of "the embodiment of God's will."[4]

Twain saw the forces of established Eastern "idealizing culture," of American genteel society, as leagued against the culture represented by his own vernacular literature. He explicitly contradicts three spokesmen for gentility, "the Professor of English Literature in Yale, the Professor of English Literature in Columbia, and Wilkie Collins" (93–94). In doing so, Twain thumbs his nose at anyone who might interpret the literary endeavor as having as its overriding purpose a presentation of an "embodiment of God's will" rather than a deeply felt and imagined construction of observed reality. He thereby gave implicit (maybe explicit) offense to most nineteenth-century American readers who took very seriously the "embodiment of God's will" approach to literature. The ambitious program behind the anti-genteel literature being produced by such wide-ranging creators as Whitman, Dickinson, James, Stephen Crane, and Twain himself was not embraced by most of those who wrote literary criticism of any sort.

Quite apart from such polemical undercurrents, the vituperative quality of Twain's prose makes "Fenimore Cooper's Literary Offences" great fun to read now. Most of us have not returned as adult readers to Cooper's Leatherstocking tales, and therefore have not reread the saga of Natty Bumppo for its evocation of the American wilderness and its wonderful ambivalence toward what Natty calls the "devilments" of progressive civilization: churches, schools, courthouses, clearings.[5] But even those who have, so long as they also remember the boredom of a forced march through the Leatherstocking series, under the incomprehensible prodding of a relentless high school teacher, cannot but howl with joy at Twain's distorted and often untrue (but often not!) accounting of those hilarious "literary offences." Twain's fun was on behalf of a literary honesty he found betrayed by the literature that Cooper represented. Professors Lounsbury (Yale) and Matthews (Columbia) were very big guns in those days, and their enshrinement of Natty Bumppo struck Twain as a deep threat to the continuing existence of Huck Finn, Hank Morgan, and other embodiments of the America that concerned him. But oblique, not direct, attack suited both Twain's purpose and Twain's poses. Even a short list of twentieth-century academic writers who have accepted Twain's version of Cooper as accurate even where it is not suggests that that which delights us can also shape our thinking, even without our awareness.[6]

And what are these poses, and what purpose lies behind them? One of the large contrasts that readers of Twain repeatedly enjoy is the Master's stance toward the respectable genteel culture of his day: on the one hand, he mocks propriety and its upholders; on the other, he clamors at their gates (his personal lifestyle, the conspicuous Hartford mansion), or at least writes as if he wants their acceptance. Part of the pleasure in the essays of this volume comes from watching our author assume first one and then another literary mask or personality: sometimes it's that of the almost simpleminded rube who understands little (see Twain's masterfully inept "translation" of his own jumping frog story from French into English); sometimes the knowledgeable, experienced "old Greyback from Wayback"[7] is in command ("Fenimore Cooper's Literary Offences"). These, and the other essays, have in common the mark of Mark the ordinary man, whose irritations are our own but whose ability to register them leaves us delighted, and then perhaps envious, but not too envious. He makes his method and manner seem so natural, so obvious and unlabored, that we feel sure we could do the same if we cared to try.

These pieces present us with Mark Twain the popular writer, one whose impulses are well intentioned and uncomplicated, whose intelligence and taste stay comfortably within the limits of a low- to middlebrow readership, and whose informal education threatens the self-esteem of no one. He plays the part that at times it galled him to play, but he plays it well, seemingly at ease within invisible constraints.[8] This is the Mark Twain who deceives us — to our delight — again and again. What daring! What nerve! Why, just watch in "Cooper's Literary Offences" as our beloved untutored Westerner takes on the social and cultural heavyweights of New York and London, of Atlantic culture. But he does so oh-so-lightly. He appreciated heavy-duty commentary, and wrote a fair amount. In this volume, however, we find nothing stronger than the peripheral fun and games of "Travelling with a Reformer." Although this piece seems mild in the context of the systemic social ills presented in *A Connecticut Yankee*, it has the qualities of its defects. That is, it allows, even encourages, readers to feel virtuous in contemplating their own future appropriation of the reformer's methods. The "force" of the good major may be beyond most of us, but Twain shows us that there is plenty of scope for pleasantly mendacious "diplomacy," should we care to try some. And how pretty to think that even our humble selves can bring some improvement to this troubled world.

But here, as with "Private History of the 'Jumping Frog' Story" and "Mental Telegraphy Again," one does not think too long or too troubledly about any greatly serious implications. "Private History" — in part, a recycling of some of "The Jumping Frog, in English. Then in French. Then Clawed Back into a Civilized Language Once More by Patient, Unremunerated Toil," from *Sketches, New and Old* — offers us, today, a double surprise: first, Twain's own surprise (as revealed in the sketch) at Professor Van Dyke's discovery of Twain's apparent unconscious plagiarism of "Jumping Frog," and then the reversal (as revealed by modern scholarship) when Twain learned some time later that the Greek version of the story, found by Van Dyke in Arthur Sidgwick's *An Introduction to Greek Composition, with Exercises*, far from being authentically ancient, was Sidgwick's own adaptation, for the textbook, of Twain's story.[9]

Perhaps equally interesting to readers familiar with the frog story of the 1860s and 1870s, Twain here uses only part of what "good-natured, garrulous old Simon Wheeler" has to say about Jim Smiley, his compulsion to gamble, and the odd but engaging creatures on whose prowess he would wager. Furthermore, in both this version and the "Clawed Back" one, Twain omits the narrative frame, probably because the standard English in which he casts himself as an earnest seeker of information concerning the nonexistent Reverend Leonidas W. Smiley presented no problem for the French translator. In any case, one misses the jest on Twain as pompously genteel outsider, caring only for dry facts and inconsiderately walking away when Wheeler begins a further yarn.

> "Well, thish-yer Smiley had a yaller one-eyed cow that didn't have no tail, only jest a short stump like a bannanner, and — "
>
> However, lacking both time and inclination, I did not wait to hear about the afflicted cow, but took my leave.

Generations of readers have wondered in vain about that cow, and have laughingly cursed the entertaining obtuseness of the story's educated narrator, whose stuffiness prevails over all. Although he excludes this conclusion here, Twain generously provides a different joke — three jokes, really — so that purchasers of the 1897 volume will receive their money's worth: first, the matter of plagiarism; then, the vagaries of the French language and Twain's magnificently fractured retranslation from same; third, the "solution" to the puzzle of why the story failed to have its expectedly fatal effect when it was published in the *Revue des Deux Mondes* (or the "Review of Some Two Worlds," as Twain had translated the journal's title in "Clawed Back").

"Mental Telegraphy Again" (a follow-up to the much longer "Mental Telegraphy," first published in *Harper's Monthly* for December of 1891 and then in *The £1,000,000 Bank-Note and Other Stories* in 1893) suggests Twain's interest both in the subject itself and in cashing in on the popular interest in psychic and spiritualistic phenomena in the late nineteenth century. We can leave problems of statistically significant sampling to others as we enjoy, uncritically, the delightful, psychologically reassuring stories here presented as evidence for what would later be called extrasensory perception. That Lieutenant H. encountered openhearted trust and kindness from the father of Miss Porter's future student acquires significance because Mark Twain, so often the professional pessimist about human nature, makes it the capstone of his article. At the very least, here is more of Twain's infinite variety.

Although most of these essays — with the grand exception of Twain's facetious attack on Professors Matthews and Lounsbury — seem to have caused little or no stir when they appeared, two triggered vigorous rebuttal, in one case ("What Paul Bourget Thinks of Us") explicit, in the other ("In Defence of Harriet Shelley") covert. Originally serialized in three consecutive issues of the *North American Review* in 1894, Twain's "Defence" exposes the stylistic, logical, and chivalric shortcomings of Professor Edward Dowden's treatment of Percy Shelly's first wife, Harriet, in Dowden's massive two-volume study of the poet, published in 1886. Twain's objections to Dowden's discussion of Harriet are many, but chief among them seems to be the professor's lack of chivalry toward the dead, and therefore defenseless, young woman. Particularly, and above all, Twain deplores Dowden's innuendoes concerning Harriet's sex life, and his repetition of Shelley's unsubstantiated charge that his wife had been unfaithful to him in 1814, thereby all but driving him into the arms of Mary Godwin.

In 1909, Dowden published a one-volume edition of his life of Shelley in which, at least to judge from various revisions, he silently accepted many of Twain's strictures on the biography's slanted language and even changed some of the wording that had led Twain to characterize the 1886 edition as "a literary cake-walk" (17). For instance, although Dowden had said in 1886, "No one who was not a partisan would assert that Harriet was not innocent," these meeching negatives did not undo the harm of his seeming effort at fairness on the preceding page: "It is no part of this biography to justify Shelley in all his words and deeds. . . . Still less is it the part of Shelley's biographer to cast a shadow upon the memory of Shelley's first wife. In many instances Shelley erred in his judgment of men and things; he may have erred here."[10] Twain no doubt exploded at the insufficiency of the "may." In the 1909 edition, perhaps in response to Twain, Dowden omitted "in all his words and deeds" from the first quoted sentence, as well as all of the last sentence — including, of course, "he may have erred here."[11]

But the most interesting change Dowden made in 1909 was to tell more rather than less about Harriet's death. In 1886 he had had full documentation for the details he chose to omit when he wrote, ". . . [Harriet's] body was found in the Serpentine river; on her finger was a valuable ring."[12] In the later edition he wrote, ". . . her body was found in the Serpentine river. She had been far advanced in her pregnancy; on her finger was a valuable ring."[13] By including the information that Harriet's dead body revealed that she was pregnant by someone other than the husband who had deserted her, Dowden as good as abandoned any pretense of chivalry. It's as if he were pointing out how wrong Twain had been to accuse him of a want of gentlemanly restraint. "See how meanspirited I could have been?" he seems to say. "You think I lacked chivalry in 1886? See what I can do when I try!" Although Twain might have appreciated the unintended joke of Dowden's self-revelation, the professor's obsessive prurience might well have saddened him: perhaps if he had sprung less stingingly to poor Harriet's defense, Dowden would have omitted the damaging (by nineteenth-century standards) report of her last pregnancy.

The final two essays in this volume concern Paul Bourget (1852–1935). Not many people read Bourget these days, neither his travel literature nor his fiction. We know that Twain had read *Cosmopolis* and that he did not admire it. The novel's open presentation of adultery would have bothered him, as would its acknowledgement *in print* of the strength of sexual attraction. In the midst of "an atmosphere of corruption,"[14] moreover, Bourget sentimentalizes the power of the Catholic church as a cure for the decadence of the society he presents. In 1889, in *A Connecticut Yankee* (ch. 17), Twain had put into Hank Morgan's mouth words ostensibly in praise of the Arthurian version of that organization — "And often, in spite of me, I found myself saying, 'What would this country be without the Church?' " — but the effect, although not Hank's intent, had been clearly ironic. ("More than once," writes Hank, "I had seen a noble who had gotten his enemy at a disadvantage, stop to pray before cutting his throat; more than once I had seen a noble, after ambushing and dispatching his enemy, retire to the nearest wayside shrine and humbly give thanks, without even waiting to rob the body.") Hank may appreciate the ennobling influence of the church, but Twain focuses his reader's gaze upon the unsanctified behavior of the nobles.

No, Twain could not approve of Paul Bourget's *Cosmopolis*, nor could he stomach Bourget's treatment of America, particularly of American women, in *Outre-Mer*, published in translation in 1895 with the subtitle *Impressions of America*. Twain was living in France when Bourget's book came out there, and had been reading it as it was serialized in the French papers. In letters from Rouen in October 1894, he refers to his "wish to abuse . . . M. Paul Bourget and his idiotic 'Outre Mer,' " acknowledging that "he is too small game to go after elaborately," and then admitting, "but I kind of love small game."[15] "What Paul Bourget Thinks of Us," Twain's "abuse" of this "small game" — in the January 1895 *North American Review*, no less — led to an odd rebuttal by one "Max O'Rell" (pen name of Léon Paul Blouët), which itself led to Twain's "A Little Note to Paul Bourget." To Twain's contemporaries, the headnote's last sentence ("It is possible that the position assumed here — that M. Bourget dictated the O'Rell article himself — is untenable" [214]) would have been an exquisitely unsubtle dig in the ribs. Author of, among many other books, *Jonathan and His Continent: Rambles Through American Society* (1889) and *A Frenchman in America: Recollections of Men and Things* (1891), O'Rell was a frequent contributor to the *North American Review* and had published "French versus Anglo-Saxon Immorality" in November of 1894 and "The Petty Tyrants of America," a piece very like "Travelling with a Reformer," in 1895. Twain asserts that Bourget himself, and only Bourget, has a right to respond to his attack on *Outre-Mer*; therefore, O'Rell cannot possibly be the author of "Mark Twain and Paul Bourget"[16] (a piece critical of both, by the way) but must have taken dictation from Bourget. So one pleasure in Twain's "Little Note" is the disingenuous way he takes O'Rell to task for having the bad manners to enter into a quarrel that was not his.

O'Rell, however, has a point when at the end of his essay he accuses Twain of insufficient perceptiveness. It appears that Twain may well have gone after the easier targets in Bourget's book while missing a number of chances for good-natured fun, and also for a more profound response to substantive matters about which he, too, cared. Consider two small samples of what Twain read in *Outre-Mer* and might have developed for his own purposes. About two-thirds of the way through chapter 5, "Business Men and Business Scenes," Bourget imagines a preindustrial America, prompted by the effects of a particular sunset on the forests that border a stretch of the Mississippi River. After evoking Longfellow by name and by quoting two lines of trochaic hexameter, he turns to Twain's old favorite:

> It is in such scenes as this that one should read the now old-fashioned romances of Fenimore Cooper, which in our youth charmed us all, beyond the seas. I have just reread one of the most celebrated, *The Pathfinder*. Its style is indifferent, the plot is constructed of childishly improbable events. The characters lack analysis and depth. And yet this book possesses the first of all the virtues of a romance, — *credibility*.[17]

Bourget goes on to speak of "Leather-Stocking, who has passed into legend even in Europe." Although Twain had not yet published his essay on Cooper, he had already committed his views to paper, as a letter to Livy shows.[18] The subject was full of interest to him, and he was full of the subject. With his assertions about both "childishly improbable events" *and* "credibility,"

Bourget offered up his neck on the chopping block. Why did not Twain swing the ax?

And how could Twain have refrained from an affirmative response to Bourget's anxieties concerning American reliance on the conscious will? Twain had for years been interested in working out his own sense of the unconscious powers within human beings. As evidenced by the horrific conscience of "The Facts Concerning the Recent Carnival of Crime in Connecticut" (1876), more benignly by his "hydraulic" theory of literature, and by the mysterious tripartite psyche sketched out in his notebooks and in many of the writings unpublished in his lifetime (most notably *No. 44, The Mysterious Stranger*), the unconscious parts of the psyche had utmost importance in Twain's view. He communicates clearly enough, especially in the unpublished writings, that merely conscious impulses and insights offered insufficient guidance in the affairs of nations or of individuals, and that to rely on them was to court disaster. Paul Bourget appears to have shared this belief. He complains that American "education does not give a large enough place to the unconscious."[19] Later, at the end of his chapter "Women and Young Girls," Bourget analyzes a portrait by John Singer Sargent, remarking that in it, the artist "has shown what I have tried to express." Two pages later, in the last sentence of the chapter, Bourget insists that this portrait "of a woman whose name I do not know" reveals about America "all that which, perhaps, will one day be its destruction, but up to the present time is still its greatness — a faith in the human Will, absolute, unique, systematic, and indomitable."

As D. H. Lawrence spelled out at much greater length in *Studies in Classic American Literature* (1923), to rely on the totally conscious determinations of will is to ignore the greater force and importance of underlying human passions and intuitions. The will-induced disasters of the twentieth century — Lawrence's first readers would have thought immediately of the First World War — suggest that the regard Bourget and Twain shared for the powers of the unconscious was a valid one. But why did Twain refrain from commenting on the matter? He is clear enough about the impossibility that any foreigner could get beyond "the exteriors of a nation" and "report its interior —

its soul, its life, its speech, its thought" (186). These interior matters become available only through what Twain calls "absorption; years and years of intercourse with the life concerned; of living it." He comes, unsurprisingly enough, to the conclusion that only "the native novelist" can get at "the souls and the life of a people" because "one learns peoples through the heart, not the eyes or the intellect." But Twain never turns this position into a thoughtful analysis of what today seems an inherent contradiction between Bourget's respect for the unconscious and the very effort upon which he was engaged.

To plunge into these waters — in print — Twain would have had to sacrifice one of his most marketable assets: his persona, his mask. He would have had to give up the pose of an ignoramus, unintellectual and even anti-intellectual, whose self-taught skills might include the ability to "claw" a story back into ridiculously unidiomatic English through an ignorance of the idioms of French, but who could never indulge seriously in analytical thought. And although he might defend a woman's virtue, attack an author's idiocy, and protest when ordinary citizens were insulted by railroad conductors and ticket agents, he would do so only on the basis of the same visceral common sense that all of his readers shared.

If we approach these essays with a view of the self-set limits of the Twain persona, we may find it sad that he so often drew back from direct presentation of his more thoughtful self. But we may also find remarkable how many different sorts of insight these eight essays provide, how clearly they reflect a wide range of interests, and what enjoyable reading they remain.

NOTES

1. In *Mark Twain in Eruption*, ed. Bernard DeVoto (New York: Harper and Brothers, 1940), pp. 223–24. The ensuing quotations from the "recited" version follow in *Mark Twain in Eruption*.

2. Twain worked out such ideas in numerous manuscripts, most notably those concerning a "Mysterious Stranger," one of his major preoccupations during and beyond the late 1890s.

3. *The Autobiography of Mark Twain*, ed. Charles Neider (New York: Harper and Brothers, 1959), p. 265.

4. Timothy Titcomb [pseudonym of Josiah G. Holland], *Lessons in Life: A Series of Familiar Essays* (New York: Charles Scribner's Sons, 1893), p. 286 (from "The Poetic Test," pp. 284–97, unchanged from the editions of 1861 and 1881).

5. *The Prairie* (1827), chapter 23.

6. For such a list, see Sydney J. Krause, *Mark Twain as Critic* (Baltimore: Johns Hopkins University Press, 1967), pp. 146–47.

7. As Hank Morgan says, ironically, of the King, in *A Connecticut Yankee*, chapter 31.

8. He felt that he gave in too often to the many editors and readers who "require[d] a 'humorist' to paint himself stripèd & stand on his head every fifteen minutes." *Mark Twain–Howells Letters*, ed. Henry Nash Smith and William M. Gibson (Cambridge: Harvard University Press, 1960), 1:49.

9. *Mark Twain: Collected Tales, Sketches, Speeches, and Essays: 1891–1910*, ed. Louis J. Budd (New York: Library of America, 1992), Budd's note on p. 1022.

10. Edward Dowden, LL.D., *The Life of Percy Bysshe Shelley, in Two Volumes* (London, 1886), 1:428–29.

11. Dowden (1909), p. 239.

12. Dowden (1886), 2:64.

13. Dowden (1909), p. 332.

14. *Cosmopolis* (Paris, 1892), p. 360.

15. Quoted in Alan Gribben, *Mark Twain's Library: A Reconstruction* (Boston: G. K. Hall, 1980), 1:79.

16. *North American Review* 161, no. 460 (March 1895): 302–10.

17. *Outre-Mer: Impressions of America* (1894; New York: Charles Scribner's Sons, 1895), p. 145.

18. Krause, p. 140, fn. 9.

19. *Outre-Mer*, p. 323.

FOR FURTHER READING

Pascal Covici, Jr.

For Twain's awareness of various ways in which humorous stories were being told and written in nineteenth-century America, the following three books offer useful and interesting interpretations: Henry Nash Smith, *Mark Twain: The Development of a Writer* (Cambridge: Harvard University Press, 1962); David E. E. Sloane, *Mark Twain as a Literary Comedian* (Baton Rouge: Louisiana State University Press, 1979); and Pascal Covici, Jr., *Mark Twain's Humor: The Image of a World* (Dallas: Southern Methodist University Press, 1962).

For short commentaries on each of the essays in this volume, as well as for views of almost every imaginable facet of Twain's life and letters, consult *The Mark Twain Encyclopedia*, ed. J. R. LeMaster and James D. Wilson (New York: Garland Publishing, 1993).

Several of the essays in this volume involve Mark Twain's responses as a reader. Alan Gribben, *Mark Twain's Library: A Reconstruction*, 2 vols. (Boston: G. K. Hall, 1980), throws light on Twain's reading and on what he made of it. Sydney J. Krause, *Mark Twain as Critic* (Baltimore: Johns Hopkins University Press, 1967), explores Twain's more formal responses to his reading.

For a useful sense of some of the uncompleted works that absorbed Twain's interest during and after the period when he wrote the material in this volume, three collections, all published by the Mark Twain Project (Berkeley: University of California Press), offer an excellent start: *Mark Twain's Which Was the Dream? and Other Symbolic Writings of the Later Years*, ed. John S. Tuckey (1966); *Mark Twain's Mysterious Stranger Manuscripts*, ed. William M. Gibson (1969); and *Mark Twain's Fables of Man*, ed. John S. Tuckey (1972).

A NOTE ON THE TEXT

Robert H. Hirst

This text of *How to Tell a Story and Other Essays* is a photographic facsimile of a copy of the first American edition dated 1897 on the title page. Although books printed from the first edition plates were manufactured until at least 1905, the earliest copies of the first edition were published in April 1897; two copies were deposited with the Copyright Office on April 9 (*BAL* 3449). The original volume reproduced here is in the collection of the Mark Twain House in Hartford, Connecticut (810/C625how/c. 1).

THE MARK TWAIN HOUSE

The Mark Twain House is a museum and research center dedicated to the study of Mark Twain, his works, and his times. The museum is located in the nineteen-room mansion in Hartford, Connecticut, built for and lived in by Samuel L. Clemens, his wife, and their three children, from 1874 to 1891. The Picturesque Gothic-style residence, with interior design by the firm of Louis Comfort Tiffany and Associated Artists, is one of the premier examples of domestic Victorian architecture in America. Clemens wrote *Adventures of Huckleberry Finn*, *The Adventures of Tom Sawyer*, *A Connecticut Yankee in King Arthur's Court*, *The Prince and the Pauper*, and *Life on the Mississippi* while living in Hartford.

The Mark Twain House is open year-round. In addition to tours of the house, the educational programs of the Mark Twain House include symposia, lectures, and teacher training seminars that focus on the contemporary relevance of Twain's legacy. Past programs have featured discussions of literary censorship with playwright Arthur Miller and writer William Styron; of the power of language with journalist Clarence Page, comedian Dick Gregory, and writer Gloria Naylor; and of the challenges of teaching *Adventures of Huckleberry Finn* amidst charges of racism.

David Bradley received a B.A. in creative writing from the University of Pennsylvania in 1972, and an M.A. in United States Studies from the University of London in 1974. He is the author of two novels, *South Street* (1975) and *The Chaneysville Incident* (1981), which was awarded the 1982 PEN/Faulkner Prize and an Academy Award from the American Academy and Institute of Arts and Letters. His nonfiction has appeared in such publications as *Esquire, Redbook,* the *New York Times,* the *Los Angeles Times,* and the *New Yorker.* A recipient of fellowships from the John Simon Guggenheim Foundation and the National Endowment for the Arts, he is currently completing a nonfiction book, *The Bondage Hypothesis: Meditations on Race, History and America.*

Pascal Covici, Jr., E.A. Lilly Professor of English at Southern Methodist University in Dallas, Texas, holds B.A., M.A., and Ph.D. degrees from Harvard University. He is the author of *Mark Twain's Humor: The Image of a World* (1962), and the editor of *The Viking Portable John Steinbeck* (1971) and *Stephen Crane: The Red Badge of Courage and Other Stories* (1991). He has served as president of the Mark Twain Circle of America. His latest work, *Humor and Revelation in American Literature: The Puritan Connection,* is scheduled for publication in late 1996 by the University of Missouri Press. He lives in Dallas and in Wilton, New Hampshire.

Shelley Fisher Fishkin, professor of American Studies and English at the University of Texas at Austin, is the author of the award-winning books *Was Huck Black? Mark Twain and African-American Voices* (1993) and *From Fact to Fiction: Journalism and Imaginative Writing in America* (1985). Her most recent book is *Lighting Out for the Territory: Reflections on Mark Twain and American Culture* (1996). She holds a Ph.D. in American Studies from Yale University, has lectured on Mark Twain in Belgium, England, France, Israel, Italy, Mexico, the Netherlands, and

Turkey, as well as throughout the United States, and is president-elect of the Mark Twain Circle of America.

Robert H. Hirst is the General Editor of the Mark Twain Project at The Bancroft Library, University of California at Berkeley. Apart from that, he has no other known eccentricities.

ACKNOWLEDGMENTS

There are a number of people without whom The Oxford Mark Twain would not have happened. I am indebted to Laura Brown, senior vice president and trade publisher, Oxford University Press, for suggesting that I edit an "Oxford Mark Twain," and for being so enthusiastic when I proposed that it take the present form. Her guidance and vision have informed the entire undertaking.

Crucial as well, from the earliest to the final stages, was the help of John Boyer, executive director of the Mark Twain House, who recognized the importance of the project and gave it his wholehearted support.

My father, Milton Fisher, believed in this project from the start and helped nurture it every step of the way, as did my stepmother, Carol Plaine Fisher. Their encouragement and support made it all possible. The memory of my mother, Renée B. Fisher, sustained me throughout.

I am enormously grateful to all the contributors to The Oxford Mark Twain for the effort they put into their essays, and for having been such fine, collegial collaborators. Each came through, just as I'd hoped, with fresh insights and lively prose. It was a privilege and a pleasure to work with them, and I value the friendships that we forged in the process.

In addition to writing his fine afterword, Louis J. Budd provided invaluable advice and support, even going so far as to read each of the essays for accuracy. All of us involved in this project are greatly in his debt. Both his knowledge of Mark Twain's work and his generosity as a colleague are legendary and unsurpassed.

Elizabeth Maguire's commitment to The Oxford Mark Twain during her time as senior editor at Oxford was exemplary. When the project proved to be more ambitious and complicated than any of us had expected, Liz helped make it not only manageable, but fun. Assistant editor Elda Rotor's wonderful help in coordinating all aspects of The Oxford Mark Twain, along with literature editor T. Susan Chang's enthusiastic involvement with the project in its final stages, helped bring it all to fruition.

I am extremely grateful to Joy Johannessen for her astute and sensitive copyediting, and for having been such a pleasure to work with. And I appreciate the conscientiousness and good humor with which Kathy Kuhtz Campbell heroically supervised all aspects of the set's production. Oxford president Edward Barry, vice president and editorial director Helen McInnis, marketing director Amy Roberts, publicity director Susan Rotermund, art director David Tran, trade editorial, design and production manager Adam Bohannon, trade advertising and promotion manager Woody Gilmartin, director of manufacturing Benjamin Lee, and the entire staff at Oxford were as supportive a team as any editor could desire.

The staff of the Mark Twain House provided superb assistance as well. I would like to thank Marianne Curling, curator, Debra Petke, education director, Beverly Zell, curator of photography, Britt Gustafson, assistant director of education, Beth Ann McPherson, assistant curator, and Pam Collins, administrative assistant, for all their generous help, and for allowing us to reproduce books and photographs from the Mark Twain House collection. One could not ask for more congenial or helpful partners in publishing.

G. Thomas Tanselle, vice president of the John Simon Guggenheim Memorial Foundation, and an expert on the history of the book, offered essential advice about how to create as responsible a facsimile edition as possible. I appreciate his very knowledgeable counsel.

I am deeply indebted to Robert H. Hirst, general editor of the Mark Twain Project at The Bancroft Library in Berkeley, for bringing his outstanding knowledge of Twain editions to bear on the selection of the books photographed for the facsimiles, for giving generous assistance all along the way, and for providing his meticulous notes on the text. The set is the richer for his advice. I would also like to express my gratitude to the Mark Twain Project, not only for making texts and photographs from their collection available to us, but also for nurturing Mark Twain studies with a steady infusion of matchless, important publications.

I would like to thank Jeffrey Kaimowitz, curator of the Watkinson Library at Trinity College, Hartford (where the Mark Twain House collection is kept), along with his colleagues Peter Knapp and Alesandra M. Schmidt, for having been instrumental in Robert Hirst's search for first editions that could be safely reproduced. Victor Fischer, Harriet Elinor Smith, and especially Kenneth M. Sanderson, associate editors with the Mark Twain Project, reviewed the note on the text in each volume with cheerful vigilance. Thanks are also due to Mark Twain Project associate editor Michael Frank and administrative assistant Brenda J. Bailey for their help at various stages.

I am grateful to Helen K. Copley for granting permission to publish photographs in the Mark Twain Collection of the James S. Copley Library in La Jolla, California, and to Carol Beales and Ron Vanderhye of the Copley Library for making my research trip to their institution so productive and enjoyable.

Several contributors — David Bradley, Louis J. Budd, Beverly R. David, Robert Hirst, Fred Kaplan, James S. Leonard, Toni Morrison, Lillian S. Robinson, Jeffrey Rubin-Dorsky, Ray Sapirstein, and David L. Smith — were particularly helpful in the early stages of the project, brainstorming about the cast of writers and scholars who could make it work. Others who participated in that process were John Boyer, James Cox, Robert Crunden, Joel Dinerstein, William Goetzmann, Calvin and Maria Johnson, Jim Magnuson, Arnold Rampersad, Siva Vaidhyanathan, Steve and Louise Weinberg, and Richard Yarborough.

Kevin Bochynski, famous among Twain scholars as an "angel" who is gifted at finding methods of making their research run more smoothly, was helpful in more ways than I can count. He did an outstanding job in his official capacity as production consultant to The Oxford Mark Twain, supervising the photography of the facsimiles. I am also grateful to him for having put me in touch via e-mail with Kent Rasmussen, author of the magisterial *Mark Twain A to Z*, who was tremendously helpful as the project proceeded, sharing insights on obscure illustrators and other points, and generously being "on call" for all sorts of unforeseen contingencies.

I am indebted to Siva Vaidhyanathan of the American Studies Program of the University of Texas at Austin for having been such a superb research assistant. It would be hard to imagine The Oxford Mark Twain without the benefit of his insights and energy. A fine scholar and writer in his own right, he was crucial to making this project happen.

Georgia Barnhill, the Andrew W. Mellon Curator of Graphic Arts at the American Antiquarian Society in Worcester, Massachusetts, Tom Staley, director of the Harry Ransom Humanities Research Center at the University of Texas at Austin, and Joan Grant, director of collection services at the Elmer Holmes Bobst Library of New York University, granted us access to their collections and assisted us in the reproduction of several volumes of The Oxford Mark Twain. I would also like to thank Kenneth Craven, Sally Leach, and Richard Oram of the Harry Ransom Humanities Research Center for their help in making HRC materials available, and Jay and John Crowley, of Jay's Publishers Services in Rockland, Massachusetts, for their efforts to photograph the books carefully and attentively.

I would like to express my gratitude for the grant I was awarded by the University Research Institute of the University of Texas at Austin to defray some of the costs of researching The Oxford Mark Twain. I am also grateful to American Studies director Robert Abzug and the University of Texas for the computer that facilitated my work on this project (and to UT systems analyst Steve Alemán, who tried his best to repair the damage when it crashed). Thanks also to American Studies administrative assistant Janice Bradley and graduate coordinator Melanie Livingston for their always generous and thoughtful help.

The Oxford Mark Twain would not have happened without the unstinting, wholehearted support of my husband, Jim Fishkin, who went way beyond the proverbial call of duty more times than I'm sure he cares to remember as he shared me unselfishly with that other man in my life, Mark Twain. I am also grateful to my family — to my sons Joey and Bobby, who cheered me on all along the way, as did Fannie Fishkin, David Fishkin, Gennie Gordon, Mildred Hope Witkin, and Leonard, Gillis, and Moss

Plaine — and to honorary family member Margaret Osborne, who did the same.

My greatest debt is to the man who set all this in motion. Only a figure as rich and complicated as Mark Twain could have sustained such energy and interest on the part of so many people for so long. Never boring, never dull, Mark Twain repays our attention again and again and again. It is a privilege to be able to honor his memory with The Oxford Mark Twain.

Shelley Fisher Fishkin
Austin, Texas
April 1996